Ou

on

Insight

A Collection
of Poetry

MW01120594

Daniel J. Mocadlo

credo
house publishers

outlookoninsight.com | outlookoninsight@yahoo.com

Published by Credo House Publishers, a division of Credo Communications, LLC, Grand Rapids, Michigan; www.credohousepublishers.com.

ISBN: 978-1-935391-84-5

Cover and interior design: Nicole Ricks

Contents

Note to the Reader

THANK YOU for spending your hard-earned money on my first literary venture. This has been written with the intention of enlightening your heart to something today's world seems to be lacking. I'll refer to it here as "absolute truth." Yes, there is such a truth, and yes, it is still available today, to those who earnestly seek it. My hope is that these pages will speak to your heart and arouse your mind. For anyone in need of nourishment—or for any who may seem in need of nothing—this book aims to share some insight.

I find myself convicted to share with you the same truth that has set me free. Inside this book I offer many questions and answers that pertain to our very existence. What I have discovered has completely changed my outlook on everything that matters.

Set in poetic style, I aimed to string together these individual pieces to suggest a familiar story or maybe an imaginative journey of a young man's search. Yet I'm addressing men and women alike. Although in the beginning I don't hone in on a particular topic, as the pages turn the story develops: a log of the "character's" questioning search for companionship and his longing for success and fulfillment. I try to expose his poor decision making, personal struggles, mistakes, and search for comfort and security.

My challenge to you: don't set this volume down halfway through. In its reflection of life the tone may at times seem dark and depressing, but it increasingly picks up momentum, until in the end it exudes purpose, meaning, and truth. Enjoy!

A Hopeful Journey

Everyone shares a common thought
Going back through time to think it:
We could have done things so much better!

Yesterday's gone;
Did I learn for tomorrow?
Odds are today is not my last.
Will I yield to hope and trust
Not to beg and not to borrow?

I work to be the pavement
For someone else's way,
Perhaps reveal a brand new light
For another's darkened day:
There's more to life than sorrow!

And if I may be so bold:
We are all daily growing old.
I'll share a journey if I may,
One implied in an abstract way.
With that being said
What then shall I say?

Call to Righteousness

Writing is like fishing:
I can take fifty casts
Before getting a bite,
Or write five hundred lines
By the end of the night,
Hoping there's one that shines,
One that's never been heard,
Not yet—but a million times;
There is power in the word.

I'll hardly be remembered
Acting confident and strong.
But when I fall short I raise the bar
Writing my personal song.
I should pick up my old guitar,

Maybe cry out a melody:
How I feel when all goes wrong,
How I try so hard to fit in
When still in the end I don't belong.
Sounds like a country song—
Grab a drink and come along.

Bring a teardrop, maybe two;
Tonight I'll cry and think of you
And what this life has put us through.
I still carry unwilling pain
Beyond the early morning rain.

This world is such a mess
And I've failed so many tests.
When my mood is down, I wear a frown;
Waiting on dreams just takes too long—
Maybe another country song.

I need to do my part
To make this old world right.
Yes, I want to do my part
But it won't be tonight.
How can I correct the wrongs
That always draw me in?
I'll write some good country songs—
That's where I can begin.

My opinion stands alone.
That's how it seems to be,
So long and far away from home—
The system versus me.
This distance is so vast:
What we have, what is gone—
Will this great country last?
Who defines how long is long?
(Questions for a country song).

We've shared with all
Who've wished to learn
We've brought them all along.
But now our bridges
Slowly burn
(I never thought this would be a song).

In the dark of night we forget
That which lightens up the day:
It can be how we act,
It can be what we say.

The special few, caught in the crowd,
Their essence is so strong.
They don't have to scream so loud;
Just how can they stand out?
By singing a loyal country song.

Please never say I didn't care;
I'm right where I belong.
The call is there for all of us:
Let's do our share, bring peace along—
Together write the lyrics—
Stand up, sing this country's song!

Battle Against Time Itself

I'm wrestling something annoying
That's not a real threat per se:
Day in and out we've struggled
Since we first met that day.
I'm always being pushed to go
And always hearing that I'm slow.
Our partnership I still regret,
Our history I can't forget.

I swear it's all because of you
I can't squeeze in all I need to do.
I'm behind you every time I look.
You don't replace what it was you took.
Yet you'll keep runnin' up on me
Swearing that you don't cheat me
But I know you simply do—
I'm ever at the mercy of one the likes of you.

They say you're so consistent
(I know that isn't true);
You keep on rolling to the next
To-do list to get through.
You steal my precious Sundays,
Quickly turning them to Mondays.
Wishing I had less time alone
But then at last you point to nine—
Can I finally make it home?

Just who made you the essence
Of my every single day?

Who asked you for your presence?
(But you'll be here anyway.)
Who gave you my permission
To send me home so late?
I miss my life but have to wait;
Who tells you that I can't slow down
When gravity steps to the plate?

I just can't seem to place the blame
On anyone but you;
There's no one else who seems to care.
I wish that I could sue—
I'd file a lawsuit, me against time
And the clock that keeps it too.

It seems time always owns me,
Has me wrapped around its hands,
Never asking and unforgiving;
I abide by its selfish demands.

A Talk with Grandfather

It's time to get up again,
The seventh day in a row.
I'll have to hurry and beat the sun
As off to work again I go.

On my way to the job site I stretch my back
(It hurts so bad I swear).
My stomach growls—it's food I lack—
But the boss man doesn't care.

Six hours off is not enough
(Yet so many bills to pay).
My hands are numb, my feet are rough;
Will I make it through the day?

Through the smoke it's hard to see—
I'm a slave to this old foundry.
I miss my wife, I have no life,
The kids grow up without me.

I'll miss my quota, miss the mark,
Be reprimanded yet again.
It's hard to focus in the dark,
Like writing words without a pen.

If I only had the tools I need
I'd be so much more efficient.
The owner, he's so full of greed—
These conditions are insufficient.

I'm wishing I could feel my hands
(For in here, it's very cold).
I bow to unjust labor demands;
At 40 I'm feeling 80 years old.

I'm still being pushed to quit
But what else can I do?
I'll be here 'til the day I die
With no insurance, no pension too.

Management says I've got it made—
If I don't like it, there's the door!
I make them a hefty profit, but
It's not enough—they're wanting more.

A Talk with an Invalid Veteran

Young man, come sit and talk to me;
I haven't a thing to do today.
I heard the porch boards creaking
As he rocked the morning away.
I just sit out here and listen
To the wind through the old oak tree;
The bird songs beckon me to sleep
With their peaceful melody.

Until the thunder wakes me up
(From a car or from a gun).
I don't know any these folks
(Old neighbors past or gone).
I guess I'm like this old oak tree,
Deep rooted in the ground—
I won't be going anywhere
Till I hear the angels' sound.

Maybe I'd run if I still could
(I'm so misunderstood,
Knowing wrong from right and bad from good),
But I won't leave my neighborhood.

These folks have everything they want
And little that they need.
I see the base is cracking:
The streets are full of crime and greed.
I still look forward to the spring,
The beauty that new growth will bring.

It's sad how people take for granted
How we survived on what we planted
(Oh, all I've lived and seen!).

I'm just so very old—
At least that's what I'm told:
I'm outta touch and I can't see,
An outcast from society.

Yet I'm content in who I am.
My father's voice I still can hear.
His ninety years like one short day
Still ringing truly in my ear.

I'm scared of what we have become
(Is this really who we are?).
A handshake deal is dead and gone
And what was once so close seems so far.
We used to work before we'd play
And put away for a rainy day.
When family was the reason
A legacy to leave behind,
We worked so hard in every season
Deserving Sunday to unwind.

We don't raise 'em like we used to—
Who really has the time?
We're falling more and more behind.
So where's the time to just enjoy,
To recollect our history,
And the fruits of our labor, employ.

These prices rise and never fall
For greed alone is answering
This culture's hungry call.
I blame it on our government;
Our representation took the fall.

I know who's really suffering:
The working class—us all.
Politicians have neglected
What the right thing is to do;
Once they get re-elected
They'll lord it over you.

This great country, it was born
On ideals that now lie torn:
Life, freedom, happiness
And a pride that now is worn.
Seems it's always about *me*—
All *my* needs must come first!
I'll take your glass of water
To satisfy my thirst.
We steal and call it borrow,
And don't prepare for tomorrow,
Selling off our liberty
For a false security—
Our freedom taking furlough.

Calling gift of life a choice,
Silencing that righteous voice,
Morality deprived of moral,
Letting feeling trump our reason.

Style appeals, lifestyle reveals
Desire to reap in just one season.
Our neighbors we neglect,
Kids are losing their respect,
And ignorance tops intellect.

"Get outta my way!" is what they all say
If I don't speed on the freeway,
And "Get out of the line!"
If I'm short a dime;
"Commit the crime, don't serve the time;
It isn't your fault anyway.
Put it on credit and then forget it;
Be responsible another day."

"Hang anyone, just so someone's hung"—
But run away from blame,
Youth is wasted on the young;
This world's increasingly insane!

Against Government Control

If everybody thinks alike—
All points of view the same,
We'll all of us fall into line;
Come on and board the train.

Where it goes beyond the station
An uncertain destination—
Not a choice once we're on board;
Just what are we heading toward?
It's no longer a free nation!

When only the engineer knows
(Preplanned in a closed-door room)
Just when and where it goes—
For passengers certain doom!

We're allowed to disagree,
Our prerogative to question!
(Responsibility in liberty
Our *duty*, not to mention).

We're given certain rights
And able minds for thinking.
Remember freedom always fights
To keep its ship from sinking.

So many times I've bombed
But failure drove me toward success.

With hands untied I'm free,
Although I'm faced with many tests.
So stand strong for liberty;
As one we'll find sufficiency—
In union my soul rests.

Our founders fought so hard for us
To realize the dream of freedom.
Tyranny rises from liberty's dust
When history's truth fails to lead them.

Warning to free citizens; Never fall asleep!
Apathy and complacency spread cancer so deep.
A utopian course can lead to disaster,
Lest the servant become the master!

Missing the Good Old Days

Remember, there was once a time
When handiwork meant craftsmen;
Long before the assembly line
Our young lads learned from tradesmen.

Not mass-produced, our goods handmade
When handshake sealed a deal in trade.
Look, see the sculptures of the past.
Today the world just spins too fast.

Reminding us we fly by night
Pretending what we do is right,
We find no time to catch the light
Just trying not to finish last.
We seek our shelter from the stone
(The one that we ourselves have cast).

Those working hands once held the power—
The craftsmenship of those antiques,
The ones not made in just an hour!
The envious eye it still critiques
The ones who let our lives go sour,
Who settled in the valleys
Never aiming for life's peaks.

Though we heed a million voices,
Knowing not which one truly speaks.
Wisdom calls our fallen choices
All the ones a fool repeats.

Find Our Place

There's only so much time—
More for some, yes, than for others;
Yet precious still the same.
Life can be a strenuous climb.

For we all will play the game,
Just trying to stay sane,
Surviving in a world
That's filled with so much pain.

Never mind and never bother;
It always seems a struggle
Keeping our heads above the water
In a world that wants to drown us,
Wishing love would still surround us
Like a baby in the arms of mother.

Patience, still the greatest virtue
('Cause this life will try to hurt you),
Keep and guide us on our way.
For in truth we need to stay;
We'll all find our place someday.

Take the time to just unwind,
Search within and bring about
Peace of mind—it's what you'll find.
Rise above your self-made doubt.

Tired of Everyone's Lies

Well, I just don't understand it
Trying hard to figure it out,
Wishing the masses would demand it:
It's time to bring the truth about.
But you can't deny the facts,
And you can't change history;
We can't darken the light of truth,
Nor dismiss it as a mystery.

Now it's time we've had enough
Though we've said it many times.
Reality it gets so tough;
Have we learned nothing from our crimes?

Dismissing all I've learned in school
(Today again is life's first day?),
Ignoring all my parents' words
Will never send me on my way.
Where's the place where justice stays?

I'm just so tired of all these lies.
Ignoring truth to get ahead,
I knew a man who lied so much
He had no notion what he'd said.
So I make sure those who know me
Know I'm who I say I am,
Can count on me as I do them;
I long for trust that doesn't bend.

I admit to so much weakness
(Aiming to grow stronger everyday).
My conscience will breathe easier
If I do just what I say.

I'm wasting so much time
Writing words between each line.
Lies the master of today,
Starved for truth that's hard to find
On the tip of any tongue
Or in the front of any mind.

Imagine truth that's unconfined:
All our stress would melt away;
Only then we could unwind
And count on all that people say.

It's a fallen world, I have the proof
(Turn on the news tonight):
Evil on the loose without reproof—
Not caring what is right.

In time of trial we must depend
On who or what determines
Every message that we send.
I aim to always tell the truth
That simply doesn't bend.

Pleasure Versus Responsibility

Say hello to me, and I to you—
We're still the closest friends
Without beginning, without end
With a lifelong job that's never through,
Do we deny we've ever met?
Working hand in hand from day to day
With common, calm, implied respect.

Just who determines what to say?
(Your name I don't know anyway;
We have always been very close.)
Although we two can think the same
On a common but yet different plane
Our decisions differ greatly.

For one beyond a doubt is wise
And one a cut above the smart.
The one prefers to play around,
The other strives to do his part.
One is game and always eager
To tackle a giant task;
The other wants a day off,
Knowing the future becomes the past.

The one is just a dreamer
Who doubts that dreams come true.
The other knows they surely do—
Having timeless, gracious proof.
One's the keeper of directions

'Cause the other's usually lost.
One respects the highest price;
The other counts the cost.

In sleep the two of us collide
(It's one of many issues
In sharing an existence inside).
My memory it escapes me.
Guess it helps I'm not alone;
I rely on our partnership
Forever carved in stone.

One would rather give it up,
Just turn his head and walk away.
The other values patience,
Highest virtue along the way.
On the road to endless freedom,
Journey often pushed aside—
Swept away by life's dismay
(The casualty of the self-denied).

The truth we bury deep as deep,
So deep we hardly hear it.
It's pushed aside like fairy tales;
Now inequality prevails;
So hard to please our inner spirit.

Sharing a heart, leading a soul,
Keeping the spirit in control,
A partnership not well defined:
The union of the conscious
And the subconscious mind.

In Common

The first warm spring day
When winter finally goes away:
The budding blossoms all around;
The cool, sweet morning breeze
In waking up the maple trees
Conveys such a pleasing sound.
Enjoying the tune of a songbird
That has found its way back to town,
I take a breath and feel alive—

Can anyone disagree?
Why focus then on our worry?
Heavy-laden with anxiety
We long to live and prosper and
We search for liberty,
Our inner spirit to belong—
For loving, fruitful life and free.

The world shares too much in common;
Have we lost our common sense?
Perhaps we should spend some time—
Just jump the boundary of our fence.
All swearing what we know is truth:
Is there no other point of view?
Please judge me not for who I seem
And I will do the same for you.

We're really not that different:
I'm from here while you're from there;

We share the ground we walk on,
Breath and share the very air.
Though the places and the faces
Sometimes change and rearrange,
As we go through life we're learning
Daily lessons, both the same.
Why is it then we fight and hate?
Why do we want to dominate?

We're more alike than we may know.
We long for old, familiar things:
A hot meal and warm bed for the night,
The feeling that a smile brings,
An ice cold drink in the shade,
A happy home to live and play,
To put behind us our mistakes—
For each today's a brand new day!

Blue skies as far as the eye can see,
Reunion with our family,
The pride accompanying our labor,
A deed of kindness from our neighbor.

We all just want to be accepted
(For who prefers to feel rejected?)
A back slap from a friend,
Just knowing we're protected,
Will let the scars of history mend.

For Completeness

Like an infant, so tenderly meek and gentle,
Depending on trust and loving care—
Both physical and mental—
And needing special attention
(Kind and nurturing, not to mention).

A strong and meaningful touch
That says you mean so much,
Not forgetting love binds together
Now and always (let's call it forever).

When a woman's mind is made up
Her "yes" means yes, her "no" not maybe.
We give her full-time attention.
(Is this why we call her Baby?)

When she cries, in need of affection,
She pours out her heart's emotion.
More a friend than a reflection,
Designed for partnership and devotion.

I have a few good qualities;
Will she recognize just one?
I've been told that it's a wife I need—
Not good for man to be alone.

First Glance

She stops the clock
When she walks into a room.
She just can't go unnoticed:
On her all eyes are focused,
To her all ears are tuned.

Defining angelic beauty,
She's the girl I don't wanna miss,
Alive and well in my dreams
With that million dollar kiss.

She pours me a drink
And flashes that wink,
Serving it up with her smile;
Spending time in her eyes, I know,
Will always be worth the while.

Another Girl

She has passion like a child
But there's a side of her so wild;
A leader who likes to follow.
She gets mad when the day is done;
Will she be this good tomorrow?
Performing at her very best
It never satisfies;
Every day to her is another test.
There's nothing gets her surprised,
Nothing that brings out a rise;
I can see the empty in her eyes.

She's looking for something
She hasn't yet known.
Longs to jump into the ring,
Sow a seed never sown.
But how the girl can sing—
Beyond the likes of anything!

I can tell her she's the best:
To her it's just a thing.
Her emotions like a machine—
To her it's all routine,
Another boring dream.

And Another Girl

He met her by mistake,
The best and worst of all;
It took a matter of a glance,
That's when he took the fall
(No way he even had a chance;
He'd break every single law).

She had a grace beyond his every dream;
His feet just left the ground.
For in her eyes he saw that gleam
As his heart began to pound.

Their eyes met—well, more like a stare
(This never happened to her before)—
He'd been all around and everywhere;
Right away she was his and more.

He said "hello" but no words came out—
Like he's known her for a lifetime.
It was fate (could there be any doubt?),
But stealing her heart would be a crime.

She looked in him and felt his passion,
Forgetting why she was even there.
A million guys and a million lies:
He sensed the smile within her eyes
As she pulled him to a chair.

If only he could show her,
Could show her anything . . .

He longed to be the one,
The wind beneath her wing.
Imagination running wild,
Her soul just overflows
Like Christmas morning to a child.
For love is the light,
The one that forever glows.

To every finish, there's a start;
To every end a new beginning.
Each of us has an able heart
To resume and renew our living.

In here and now we have a part—
There's great power in forgiving.
It's hard to find love when led by fear
That holds stakes against our winning!

Go Out with Me!

She's a diamond in the rough—
She's still surrounded and covered—
A beauty in every sense of the word,
Displaying such telling promise
She has yet to be discovered
And her voice longs to be heard.

She sparkles like the sun,
And stars gleam in her eyes,
Holding power to make me undone
Along with a million guys—
She keeps us all on the run.
She's real as real, without disguise,
I wish to be her special one—
No way, no how: there's no surprise!

Like a bud that's ready to blossom,
Personality so wholesome
Her heart longs to be loved,
But she gives the chance to no one.
She has so much to give
Yet buries the hurt from someone,
From someone she can't forgive.

Baby, search inside your soul
And courage is what you'll find.
Then set yourself a standing goal;
I trust the wisdom in your mind.

You're stronger than you think,
More virtuous than me.
So never let your ego sink—
You're everything a woman
Could ever aspire to be!

Believe in Yourself, My Love

My love, you are a shining star
In a world that's much too dark.
Your essence is a fire
Still looking for its spark.
You have an awesome purpose
So deep and rich and pure;
But please, my Dear, believe in yourself
And that will be your cure.

I know one day you'll hit your mark;
Of that, I'm really sure!
I can see the real you.
I've found what so many just can't find;
Even with my two eyes closed
I'm far from being blind.

Surround yourself with friends—
The ones who give you strength,
The ones who really care
And listen when you share
The person you truly are.
My special, precious morning star,
May your dreams take you far!

I know the unrivaled beauty that's you
On the inside and on the out.
Just don't believe the many lies;
Your so-called friends have made you doubt.

Your powers of emotion run so deep;
You truly wear life's ups and downs.
It's okay to cry, but please don't weep—
I just can't bear your wearing frowns.

I love to see your beautiful smile,
The one that's always worth the while;
It's always in my memory
Right in the front of my back file.

That's My Girl!

I don't call it fishing
'Cause I seldom get a bite;
Instead I call it casting
And I'll try with you tonight.
It really doesn't matter
If I teach you right or wrong.
'Cause fish don't matter anyway;
It's being beside you
And seeing inside you
I've wanted all along.

Let's watch that old moon rise;
It's time it takes its place.
Can you count the stars above
Or comprehend their endless grace?
Just being alone with you
As always is so fine;
We're far from distraction,
Such real satisfaction:
You've placed your hand in mine
(Feeling righteously divine).

When the sparks started flying
There's was no denying.
(Would we be joined forever?)
With a tear she was crying:
Was I worth her endeavor?
Were we even worth the trying?

Is she the real deal?
Will she teach me how to feel?
I'm on the fence without recompense;
My inner self can I reveal?
My hungry heart does she long to steal?
Until tonight I've always had
Two hands upon the wheel.

The fish are just not biting
But the company's delighting.
So feeling the warm summer breeze
And the autumn chill alighting.

I took off my flannel shirt
And wrapped her up—it couldn't hurt.
Our attraction so inviting
A flame well worth igniting:
To her beauty I'm fully alert.

That might have been some years ago;
We still forget, but we both know
In this crazy life we're caught in.
Don't let me go, don't ever stop.
Reach for me by the hand
And remember love like ours
Holds the power to heal our scars,
And is always in demand!

The Best

She finds beauty in the little things,
The things I usually ignore:
The blessings of a brand new day
A gentle breeze felt in the shade,
Or a tiny seashell on the shore.
But the things in her I most adore . . .

Her strength and courage.
Somehow they've rubbed off on me,
Her deep faith and her help
Through times of misery
But most of all her love.
I couldn't rise above
The man I needed to be.

That's when she came along
Like a famous country song.
I've found my heart and soul;
I'm right where I belong.

She alone can find the good
In me when I've been bad.
She can tell by lookin' in my eyes
The kind of day I've had.
And she holds the remedy
For all that's ailin' me.

She's the reason I wake with a smile,
Nothing else I'm needing more.
If I am guilty, put me on trial
For loving the girl I adore.

I Put Faith in You and Me

Everything is relative—
Reaction follows action,
And gravity pulls up to down
With little satisfaction.

Power is force times distance,
And friction needs two things,
Matter simply takes up space,
And labor isn't done by kings.

Roll a ball and there it goes;
It rolls till something stops it.
Physical laws, yet how many know
The designer Who's behind it?

Don't we all just want some fun?
A smile is still contagious.
Love is best when two are one;
Without that it's outrageous.

Positive draws negative
For opposites attract.
We're different but equal;
That truth is just a fact.

Loyalty is hard to find
Like mining buried gold.
Uncommon sense is ruling us
As wisdom's growing old.

Endurance, it will take us to
The place we need to be.
Devote yourself to us then:
Put your faith in you and me.

She Never Gives Up on Me

A pocket full of nothing
Once brought this good man down.
Out of work (oh not again!)—
The cycle's come back 'round.
I promised her a smile again
Yet left her with a frown.

I never planned for idle times
And feel I'm guilty of some crimes.
I'm back in unemployment lines,
And on the sobering ride back home
I bought my gasoline with dimes.

Amazing she's still lovin' me!
I've been hit hard upon the head
By every apple from the tree—
So hard it's hard to see.
I promised her a dream again
But I have failed so miserably.
Is it a sign of trying times—
Or is it really me?

I had to sell my clubs and say
Goodbye to the summer car.
The bass boat's gone, and with it went
My shiny new guitar.

Every time I think I'll heal
There's just more damage to reveal—
Another brand new pressing scar;
But loss of faith won't get me far.

I'm not an easy partner when
We're not living as we should,
For cutting back on hopes and dreams
Is hardly fun and can't be good.

But she won't lose her faith in me
(The truest partner endlessly):
I never will give up on us
(She knows I never could).

On evenings when she comes home mad
I know what kind of day she's had.
So sorry, I'm a stay-home dad!
Those nights when she drags in so beat
I know that it takes all she has
To stay up on her feet.

Yet I know it's not her fault,
And I don't want to put her down.
She's keeping something in the vault;
She's waiting tables back in town.

The patience she displays—
I know that it's true love!
She's the greatest gift from God
Sent down from heaven above!

She smiles so like an angel
And takes it all in stride.
She wouldn't do a single thing
To hurt my manly pride.
Despite whatever comes our way
Our love will never be denied!

I love who you are inside,
Can't forget about the out!
I know that I'll get back on track
(It's only fear that brings me doubt).
Thank you, Love: You carry my slack,
And we're what teamwork's all about!

Miracles Happen

Two seconds, like one day
(One I wish would fade away).
Not believing what's transpired:
Opinions so hard-wired.
I believe in miracles today:
A friend has kept me from harm's way,
A friend to be admired.

Was it a touch of faith,
Or yet a touch of hope?
For someone lent to me a hand.
Friendship's always in demand
But only the thankful understand.

Two seconds, like one day,
The day I still regret,
Until that miracle occurred—
The one I can't forget!

That moment time stood still
I froze on empty and got my fill,
A reaction beyond my very will
Stuck in the muddy valley,
Delivered atop the highest hill.

Two seconds, like one day;
Our first kiss, Dear, was from a dream.
Remember when you said "I do"?
The baby's eyes have got your gleam.

The storms that we have been through,
Times I feared we'd lost it all;
Imparting strength through toughest times
Just seems to be our call.

Two seconds, like a lifetime—
I can't think of losing you.
I pray, Lord, that our future
Will hold our dreams in view.

A Day Behind and a Dollar Short

My wipers have quit working
(But only when it rains)
And just today my tire went flat—
The day before its scheduled change.
I planned to put in the storm windows
Before the winter winds blow;
Now there's three inches of snow
On the frozen ground.
I hope the boss forgives me
If I ignore the alarm clock's sound.

Baby, please don't use the stove
Until the pilot's lit,
And watch out for the broken chair
Before you try to sit.
Come on now, please forgive me
When I fail to get things done;
It seems somewhere along the way
We've both forgotten to have fun.

Day in and then day out
It seems the same to me—
A day behind, a dollar short,
So much responsibility.

Please love me like you used to
When I was your big man;
I haven't gone off anywhere,
Just missed the master plan.

Remember how to make me laugh
(I know that you still do).
Don't forget what really matters:
Our hearts, Dear, must stay true.

Look deeply in my eyes
And take me by the hand,
Lay down your guard, my dear,
And help me understand.
Just join me and we'll disappear—
I'll deliver your demand.
Two as one is so much fun;
Let's make it real and not pretend.

As good as in the old days
The new ones have begun.
Let's grab our coats and Frisbee
And take the dog for a run.
Please don't forget behind the clouds
When the mood is set in gray
We can look ahead and see the sun;
Tomorrow's a brand new day!

Making Mistakes

I would think that by this point
I'd have made enough mistakes;
Somehow by now (I'm not sure how)
Our lives should just be great!
Yet I've done it again,
I've let you down:
I promised you a dream,
But I've left you with a frown.
It's really isn't me babe, can't you see?
The world's just stacked against me!

That's why pencils have erasers,
We have life rings not to sink,
Family cars have air bags,
And fences skirt the brink.
Parachutes and lifeguards
Are there for times of need.
Big toys they all have warranties,
But what in life is guaranteed?

Crutches, casts, and bandages—
Stitches if that's what it takes—
Guardrails, flags, and smoke alarms.
"Please set the emergency brakes!"
Welcome to the real world now
Where people make mistakes . . .

You're waiting on my next one;
You won't have to wait too long

'Cause time has a way of adding up
The things that I do wrong!
I try to do the best I can
(I'm just a common, simple man,
Yet complex beyond belief).
If I could figure out myself
I'd find such great relief!

Just why I act the way I do
Everyone still asks of you.
I'm sure you say that there's no way
To know me—you have not a clue.

Tired and shucking my vanity,
Struggling to keep my sanity,
A dollar short, a day behind—
I'm wound up so very tight.
Just where's the time to unwind
Or the road to make it right?

We always want what we can't have
(In perspective, we have enough).
Let's do our best with what we've got
And learn to love the simple stuff!

Simply Do

I've no time to complain, Dear,
But you know that I still do.
I should shut my mouth
When wrong words come out
And take the back seat
When I can't repeat
Everything I said I'd do.
We can't let life beat us down;
That's way too easy to do!

A partnership is hard to find—
But me and you are well defined
And Baby, I am here for you!

I'm glad you haven't given up;
You wouldn't even try.
I don't know what you see in me
And if I did, I don't know why.
We give each other all we can—
I strive to be your perfect man!

Please buy some time, Dear, cut me slack.
For I must find our hedge
To protect us from the dangers near
Before we get close to the edge!

Hold me close, then, take my hand
So our two hearts can take a stand,
Success and love together make;
Please know me only for my heart
And not for each mistake!

Don't Give Up on Us

I thought we were a team,
I thought we were a pair.
We live in the same house
And breathe the same old air.
Although I'm far from perfect
My good intentions have been there.
I'm sorry you can't wait, but Love,
Don't leave me, don't you dare!

Just hold on one more day
(This really isn't fair).
I'll change my childish ways
To show how much I care.
This distance that's between us
I really just can't bear;
Let's try to talk just one more time—
Let's have a seat, please take a chair.

Baby, I'm so sorry
We don't communicate;
As least I thought we did
But it's too little and too late.
I thought that we were lovers
But I can't play this game;
I'm always one step closer
To taking all the blame.

Please don't misunderstand:
I love you till the end.

And all of our special dreams
Don't have to be pretend.
Look deeply into me
As I do into you.
Come on, let's be what I still see,
The truest partners endlessly.

Let's do, then, what we do—
It's always been our best.
Let's just keep pushing through,
Confronting every test.
Although sometimes it seems
That it's not worth the fight.
We can't take us for granted;
We know that we both bite.

Deep down inside me I still know
It's not about control;
Relationships, my Dear, must flow,
Connecting soul to soul.
So Baby, take my hand
And help me understand:
Sharing love is in demand as
We won't find it everywhere.
I know we are a team;
Yes, we're a special pair.

Misunderstood Me

I've tried so very, very hard
Right to the point my heart feels scarred.
I thought I'd healed a million times
But still I'm paying for my crimes,
A sentence that I can't outrun.
I'm all caught up in misery—
What happened to having fun?

Is all I have not good enough?
I thought I was strong, Girl, strong and tough.
When did the right thing turn so wrong?
I always wanted to belong—
Here comes another sad, sad song.

The road to hell, my Dear, we know
Is paved with good intentions.
(I've played all the exceptions).
You know I'm all for "being good"—
Yet always I'm misunderstood.

Just spend a day inside my world
(I'm sorry, there's no season pass).
Nothing's planned, not much for sure,
So have a seat and raise your glass.
You know I fly by the seat of my pants—
Don't know where I am going, that's for sure;
I'm tired of the same old dance, as it were.

My core beliefs I can't conceal;
My emotions are a great big deal.

I want so much to stop and feel
A sense of loving thoughts from you—
Please never fake and always real.

Stand ground to what those others say
(They're always dropping bombs my way).
Don't give up when I don't act right;
It's just a phase, won't last the night.

Tomorrow always starts anew:
I'm left here with a lot to do
And it would sure be better
If my days included you.

Take Me Back

She moves like a ballerina
As she walks along the beach,
Arms swaying like a pendulum
But too far outta reach.

Those eyes (like the brightest angel)
Did miracles perform.
Yes, she's the one who rings my bell
And she has got the only key
To set my heart's alarm.
Without her I'm just not me—
I'll protect her from all harm.

Charm is so deceiving
And beauty is so fleeting—
Yet one last thing in common
Our hungry hearts are needing
What one day will be coming—
Good times and times of bleeding
And a time to reap the harvest
Another season after seeding.

To you, my Love, I'm pleading:
You have so much upon your plate,
But the three of us still need you
And yesterday's too late.

I wish I were a part of you,
That I could still be in your sights.
I'm here, your former soul mate, and
I'm fighting all my wrongful rights.

This really is the brand new me;
I've tested the walls of sanity.
Darling, let's take our chances,
On those rivers of romances
And challenge the course of fate.

Unlock your forgiving heart—
If I only play a better part—
My Baby, open up your gate;
For wisdom calls us, Dear, to wait.

The Power of Love

When your back's against the wall
And life's no fun at all
Will you climb out of that hole,
Find that light within your soul?

The car it won't go
Without gas, you know,
And a fridge you can't fill
If you can't pay the bill . . .
But no one really cares!

When it's dark outside,
When it's cold at night,
You're without the heat
And without your light.

Do you just climb out
Or jump back into bed?
Blankets sure feel good
When you're in the mood
To sleep away another precious day.

Do you just ignore the voices
And all the spectrum choices
From somewhere in your head?
Do you fight all those fears
Or drown 'em out with beers,
Confront the day or choose instead
To hide behind your tears?

With faith good things will happen.
Do you wish you never fell behind
And long to ride the wagon?
Now the pain inside it swallows my pride;
I should have listened when she said
"I believe in you and you know it's true;
Can't you get that through
Your stubborn head?"

Do you get up to face the daily grind,
Missing her warm embrace,
Fallin' back behind a little more
With every passing day?
For joy in life doesn't have to end;
There's a plateful on the way.

This I need to comprehend:
I'll be broke until my heart can mend.
But love I know will dominate:
Its power is much too great,
Its essence much too strong.
Each of us needs to play a part—
How else can we belong?

Missing Her

I have to find the strength
When all I feel is fear.
But nothing much comes easily
Except for that third beer—
I have to embrace love
(It seems nowhere around)
Just knowing that it's this I crave,
I'm bounced between lost and found.

I miss the times she held me tight
Content with all my weaknesses—
My Love, your love was just so right.
My guard was down in sleep at night,
Thoughts of you I kept all day.
Now, I'm bound to loneliness
Since we've had this time away.

Welcome to my home;
Let's share a drink, come in and sit;
You wouldn't want to live here,
Just a quiet place to visit
'Cause her memories thicken up the air.
We seem so far beyond repair,
Wishing that I could go back there

Before I was so bound by sin.
I have to find my old desire.
I know it's here somewhere within;
I shouldn't try to block it.

Let the journey now begin . . .
Remember, you aren't the only one
Who rarely ever feels the sun,
Its rays so soft upon your hand;
Its warmth is always in demand.

I just can't seem to understand
The passions I possess.
But they're not likely to impress;
The dreams I have may not come true,
But, Baby, they're including you!

Come back to me and you will see
We'll weather yet another storm.
It's not like it's the first alarm
And no one's always safe from harm.

What won't kill us, Dear, will make us stronger.
Does hell make heaven seem even longer
When we think we don't belong here?
And just can't sing a song here?
Tune to hear love's calling voice
Does the heart really have a choice?

Ready to Rekindle

Today, for the first time again,
Is the last chance he will have
To tell her that he loves her;
She belongs right by his side.
This is where disagreements
And deceptions come alive:
How many years, and what's too long?
Can yesterday just go away
To make today belong?

We're so like those trees in the wind,
Blowing, bending, and swaying.
But let's not break in the winds of demand;
There's power in praying and staying!

For so much time has passed—
Can we forget it ever was?
Do our minds say that it wasn't?
It's painful, yes, to remember
The times that were so pleasant.

I remember warm days of December
When family was the reason
The season brought us together.
We'd put behind what made us mad,
Be grateful for the all we had
And the things that many do not.

Should we not be thankful just the same?
What's cold to you to me is hot.

The sorrowful and bitter truth:
Where's the content for all we've got?

My Dear, I will love you forever;
I'll carry you in my heart.
Why then must we separate?
Why can't we just restart?
I guess we need a jumpstart
To our living, loving hearts!

Please take me back to that special place
Where home was the sense we knew.
Back then when love was still alive
And the moon was London blue.

Falling Apart

Why can't you see the real me?
(I'm looking right into your eyes.)
You follow what those strangers say,
Those misconceptions, bombs away!
I am real, but I can still surprise—
I only tell the smallest lies.

I always thought you knew me;
Weren't we friends right from the start?
Why would you crush my every dream
And then condemn my heart?

Struggle is what life's about—
Not much that's easy along the way—
Always searching for some way out
Because there's hardly time for play.

I'll put aside for one more day
The everything I want to do;
If you'll look deep inside my soul
I think you'll catch a clue:

I admit that I am normally not
What everyone thinks I should be;
I have my reasons and my doubts
But I'm who I need to be.

Your emotions rule your common sense,
So stop and think before you act;

Remember both sides of the fence
And know that opposites attract.

Am I a show no one wants to see,
A bad rerun, a dull comedy?
Maybe I'll catch your blind side;
When you're not looking you will see
I have a beating heart inside,
One that has lost its worldly pride,
The way that everyone's should be.

Why do you make me feel this way?
Am I the one you want to hurt?
Just a reflection in the mirror
To smother me within the dirt—
The side of me that you won't see,
The side that's so much clearer—
If you would open up your eyes
I'm more about love, not terror.

Use your reason, put aside emotion,
Look hard to find the real me
Instead of tossing me out to sea
To be swallowed by the ocean.

You're relying on sight, not inner vision;
I must live my life, perform my mission.
Oh sure, I'd rather grab my pole,
Do what I love—that's fishing!
Instead I'm wasting precious time
Becoming what you're wishing!

Imagine

His heart is all that he has left,
The last thing left to lose.
For he's already given everything else
(Those facts don't make the news).

He thought that he could change her
(She thought she could change him too),
But now he hears the sorrowful sound
Of their differing points of view.

They are what make the world go 'round:
We're allowed to disagree,
But where's respect, integrity?
It's where diversity is found.

Just when did want turn into need?
For she grew to expect
What she used to desire.
Throwing him like a dead log
Straight into the fire.

He just couldn't understand
(He tried to do his best);
Guess he misread her real plan
And failed her every test.

When he looked into his heart
Was it she he really saw,
Or just the mirror's reflection,
Hanging on the wall?

He knows she'll never comprehend
The reasons he must leave
To save what's left of his spirit.
But nobody listens to hear it—
There's plenty of time ahead to grieve.

He feels the dark outside
And wears the cold at night;
Now away from the heat
And far from the light.

He longs for a time
Not feeling so alone
When life will again be fun.
And there's no place like home,

Where a curly-haired beauty
With bright baby blues
Will run to the door,
Just feeling the love inside him
And only wanting more.

Into his arms she'll fall
As they become as one;
For she is all he needs—
She'll be his morning sun.

He probably will never count
Those stars within her eyes,
Hoping that he'll get the chance
(Wouldn't *that* be a pleasant surprise?)

To love again, to live and dance,
Dreaming, never growing old,
That theirs would be the story—
Lasting one that's always told.

Numb the Pain

This old bar—oh no!
It's closing time again,
Time to say goodnight,
Goodnight to my dear old friend.
Uncle Jack, please don't get mad at me;
You are my only family;
I'll see you when the sun shines again.

In the morning I will change,
Resist you maybe a minute or two,
Replace you with food for breakfast—
You don't like it when I do.

But the truth is, my old dearest friend,
You lie to me and you don't defend;
My broken life you don't care to mend.
Callin' my name at the strangest times
Like I have to square on my unpaid crimes,
Always turning my billfold into dimes.

I used to have her by my side—
The warmest touch; she'd hold my pride.
I'm scared to face how I let her go;
The truth is that I don't reveal
That which I do not really know!

It's like I woke and found her gone.
I guess she meant those things she said—
In one ear and out; her threats were long
(I'll feel better after a week in bed).

If I could just go back and give
And be ten times more sensitive;
If only I had listened
When those precious teardrops fell,
I'd be with her in paradise
Instead of here in hell.

I try to pretend I don't know you
(In fact we're closer than I thought).
You leave my tired hands tremblin';
In your web I know I'm caught.

I cannot see beyond the haze
And can't remember holidays.
What I've lived for now is all for naught;
It's all a real big blur—
Those millennium years that were.
Now I really miss her for sure!

He takes me by the hand
And helps me understand . . .

I'm not full of greed
And her love I don't need.
I can reap a full harvest, he tells me,
Without ever planting a seed.

Losing Focus

I still can't believe what I did
(I know it's just not who I am);
I guess I kept my feelings hid;
My actions I condemn.

I was at the top of my game,
Prosperity surrounding me.
But I grew temporarily insane,
Falling short of the me I expected to be.

Losing my focus and my drive
I had nothing else to prove:
Like retiring at twenty five—
No mountain I couldn't move.

What brought me to this place
Just when I had it all?
Not much left now for me to chase
From when I took the fall.

What led me down this shameful road?
Where did it all begin?
It seems I lightened up my load
To let the sin come in.

I'll trace my steps as best I can;
Did it start from being bored?
I turned into a lonely guy—
That man who had been adored!

I've always been protected;
I am a protector myself.
But I started feeling rejected
And put my heart up on a shelf.

The truth that I once held, Dear,
I left lying on the ground.
The bell would ring so loud and clear,
But now it barely makes a sound.

I held the deck and played the card,
A gambler at the table.
My loving heart, it turned so hard
I was willing but unable.

I did the deed based on my greed;
I pushed my conscience to the side;
For self-indulgence was my need—
I was overtaken by shameless pride.

Justice should be blind
But it has changed to perfect vision.
Laziness consumed my mind
And distorted my life's mission.

The truth before me I refused,
Contention turned to bitterness,
Your trust in me I then abused;
I filled you with my emptiness.

I left the door thrown open wide;
The enemy came in.

There's nothing worse; when he's inside
I expect destruction and divvy out sin.

I don't know what is left to do
Or how much worse I'll feel;
I took advantage of me and you.
My resentful heart must heal.
But where do I turn to begin?
Who'll wash away my dirt?
Can I be cleansed of all my sin?
And released from all of my hurt?

Decision Time

I'm not gonna let you perish.
Like an apple on the ground
You lie not far from the tree,
When everything you really need
Is close and all around.

You know so much better
So deep down inside,
But I haven't felt that part of you—
I've searched so far and wide.

Just blink if you can hear me;
My voice you can't ignore.
For love, it won't die easily
And I'll push to give you more.

Sadly, you've forgotten,
Like slowly the apples turn rotten.
It started with the company you keep—
I wish that you had listened!
I had a premonition
Wondering where and when you'd sleep.

Hanging out with the snakes
(You thought they were your friends),
The light you chased and had to catch
Was nothing but dead ends.

I trembled at your future
When I clearly saw your friends.
You bought the lie by which you're bound.

Daniel J. Mocadlo   69

Your spirit cries without a sound;
Each heart needs love before it mends.

Could I ever let you die?
The pain you've put me through!
You don't know up from down
Or what you need to do.

I know that you're confused now
But still I wish you'd see
That I am not a stranger,
And I never want to be.
And that's how you treat me.

How can I make you realize
(I'm staring right into your eyes)?
I'm accustomed to your fooling me,
But now I'll call your bluff;
It's time now to get better—
We've simply had enough!

I've tried to say my peace
Still holding on so tight,
My perseverance goes so far
And yet another sleepless night.

Through my tears it's hard to see
I'm doing what is right;
One day you'll walk with victory
Though tonight you face a fight!
This just may be your final chance
(I know you're black and blue).
Don't make this saving choice for me;
It's got to be for *you!*

Endless Cycle

Sometimes I speak
Just to hear myself talk;
Sometimes I stand up
To see if I can still walk.
There are days I simply think too much
About this and that and her and such,
Missing the feeling of loving touch—
Amounting to nothing at all.
It took years to build foundations
That only took a day to fall.

What's been taken away
I can't get back.
There's plenty of common sense I lack:
I wake up when I need to sleep;
I'm drowning now the water
That has always been knee deep.
I've carelessly lost
What was mine to keep;
Hindsight holds the clearest vision.
A bystander, me, to my own life's mission,
I rarely sow; how can I reap?

Just how did it happen? You tell me,
For I'm no stranger to misery.
Today I'll keep my big mouth closed
And be judged for all that's been exposed.
Fools rejoice changing history,

And I am a master of mystery—
A master of not much at all
Bringing up the rear again
As pride precedes a fall.

No Excuse

The cycle of abuse,
It really has to end!
Do we ignore the truth
And then try to pretend
That it has never happened?
Somehow it never could.
And just who can you turn to
When you're so misunderstood?

Can the pain be put to rest
And will the hurt just go away?
I long to live within a place
Where love will always stay.

It's such a shame these days
(We see it more and more)—
Passing along the anger
And always keeping score!
There is so much more to live for
That we must close this door!
We're running out of time—
There's just no victory in this war!

There's no sense in renewing
The victim we've become;
I witness my ungluing
As my stitches come undone.

Do you really even know me?
Where I come from at all?

Don't just stand there and observe me,
Watch me stumble and then fall.
Please keep my head from banging
Onto each and every wall!

You thought that you were in control,
Maneuvering it all:
You had to make yourself so big
To make me look so small!

You wanted just to keep me
With my head beneath your foot,
Telling me how I should live
My life in chains you put!
You starved my soul and spirit
And I will no longer hear it;
Don't repeat your evil lies
Or try to hide your thin disguise.

You kept me in the dark,
But I'm the one who's strong
And now I'll go where I belong.
Your insecurity shows
Bright as the light of day,
You force me by your side.
I am the source of all your pride;
I have a loving heart inside
And that is something you can't say!

I'm leaving you to start anew;
I'm done with what you've put me through.

Although I do feel sad for you
I know you'll never catch a clue
And I've got healing to go through.
And with my own eyes I will see
My struggle is reality!

Just who will buy your lies again?
You'll never hurt another!
All should beware of hidden sin:
Wolves dwell within sheep's cover.

Another heart will not be soured:
For here's your scarlet letter.
Now all will know that you're a coward;
The world is so much better!

Tired of Growing Tired

How many errors will I make
Over and then twice again?
How many times, how many crimes—
When will my brand new life begin?

I bite my tongue, I take a breath,
I close my eyes and realize
That I won't outrun death.

It's no surprise my thin disguise
Will show with light of day.
I run off every single road
I take to find my way.

How will I ever reach the stars
While living in these local bars?
They keep me down and in the dirt;
I know I've got to change my focus,
Sick and tired of self-made hurt.

I never find the answers
To all my questions why, like
What's my purpose all about?
Low on courage, full on doubt,
How and when will I find my way?
I don't know what is left to say—
I'm always looking for an out.

I'm getting tired of being tired
And keep on asking why.
I need to find who I'm born to be—
I hope, before I die.

No Security

As you can see I'm giving up—
My hands are in the air.
I know that I should push on
But I just don't want to care.

Confusion's my companion;
When I'm sure I'm here, I'm there.
Separating the truth,
Fighting over each word,
Poor opinions get turned to law—
So many laws I hadn't heard.

For I just can't make sense of it:
I'm longing for freedom and fun,
Confused by my surroundings,
Security on the run,
I'm hoping the stitches will stay together
But fighting the feeling they're coming undone.

So busy I hadn't noticed.
Working so hard to get by,
Losing touch with priority,
My passions have passed me by.

How to Reach the Sky

Just how long is time, anyway?
How far are those stars up in the sky?
I have so many questions,
So many questions why,

Like just why some are born to lead
And others always follow,
And who determines for me
What will come of my tomorrow?

I'm never noticed here
Like I used to be back there.
Inside I am a champion—
To this world just a square.

With faith, good things will happen:
A good beat to a bad song, it
Still gets my tired feet tappin'.

One day it just may happen
That I will fall in love
Just like I know I could.
For don't I still deserve it?
My soul still says I should.

To find the one beneath this sun
To share my silent dreams,
To bring about the lively things
Makes lonely days more fun.

'Cause it's a hard, hard task
With each day just to follow through
Whatever this old world can ask
Is often asked of me:
I'm asked to do some things
Of which I strongly disagree.

It's like my life is not my own;
I'm burdened with responsibility
And far off from tranquility.

It's not because of who I was
But who I'm going to be;
For even with the blindest eye
I know I'll always see.

Perhaps I'll see much clearer
Every day as time goes by,
That one fine day I'll know for sure
Just how to reach the sky.

Change

Now when I look back
On all that I am
I don't want to go back,
Make the same errors again.

Still I wouldn't change
The lessons I've learned,
The bridges I've burned.

If that to you sounds strange
Then I can't really share.
In fact reality gets tough—
Yeah, life's not always fair!

My point of view's from here
And yours from over there.
I've been dealt some cruel blows
And God only knows
The real reason why.

Many pray for one more day
While some just want to die.
Imagine there's no heaven?
I don't even want to try.

When your dreams get crushed
And your bankroll busts
And friendships pass you by,
Just look beyond the midnight sky

And try to count the stars
And all the reasons why.

We are born to bleed;
Are we born to cry?

Yeah, pain walks hand in hand
With success, with love and wisdom,
And though you try to take a stand
You can't always beat the system.

Most people we meet
Out there on the street
Give in to their defeat;
The past we still repeat.

It's a shame in a sense
But it is what it is;
It's sad that people every day
Still fall and wander and go astray.

As though lost in a trance,
They fall victims as prey
To the evil around.
Just when did we lose
Our lost and our found?

I sure hope we get more—
A lot more angels on the ground—
And love to overshadow
Evil's empowering sound.

Hard Work and Patience

For most it takes a lifetime
For lessons to be learned;
Some float right through them freely
While others just get burned.

We learn more from the hard times
Than the times we're on the top!
Without reason, with no rhymes
Our life gets complicated—
But with wisdom, maybe not!

It takes more than just a day
For things to go our way.
With hard work and with patience
We'll find time to rest and play.

Because our love walks hand in hand
It can defeat the vilest plan;
The hardest thing to do is just
To hear and understand.

When others just can't hear
The heart cry of your voice
(It comes from deep within),
Sometimes you've got no choice.

Your heart leads you along:
It can respond to any song.
You're just wanting to belong.
The weakest ones grow strong.
But lacking nourishment,
The truth may still seem wrong!

Someone Has the Answers, But Not Me

Contradiction of the heart,
Rebuking its own righteous will;
Hostile takeover of the mind,
Allowing evil to have its fill.

How did we get so desensitized,
Ignoring who we really are?
Still bypassing our own conscience
To create a brand new scar?

It's hard to recall the first time
I threw out every rule
And stepped way out of line.
Playing the part of the fool.

At first it was so hard;
I was stretched in two directions.
Ignoring my heart, I played the card,
Revealing my imperfections.

Suppressing the truth I ignored
And hurting the one's I adored.
Running from the consequence,
Falling off the integrity fence,
Rationalizing in suspense,

Living under false pretense,
My days became just too intense,
Tearing me apart,
Begging for a brand new start—
Contradiction of the heart.

Is it the thrill? Is it the rush?
Why is doing what I know is wrong
Becoming so much easier
As time drags on and on?

My sin's became a habit
And now I've got to have it.
I won't even doubt it—
I can't live without it.
My heart can cry "No!" and my mind resist.
But loss of control and confusion exist.

Just how did I get here?
I can't deny the facts:
The root of the tree
Is about to be axed.

I'm no longer me
And I'm no longer smart:
Fighting, drowning my soul,
Contradicting my heart.

I know someone has the answer—
Someone whom I don't know.
I don't want to live another day;
I know how it will go.

How far am I beyond repair?
Does someone out there give a care?
I've got a great big choice to make:
I'm searching for forgiveness
From my every mistake.

Just who, now, is this Jesus,
The one they talk about?
Is He the one who'll please us?
I'm feeling so much doubt.
But where else can I go?
(I've got nowhere left to run!)
Can there really be a God
And did He send His only Son?

The Beginning of Knowledge

My friend, don't be shy; I'm so glad you asked.
It's best to search for truth right now—
Of who and when and why and how?
Before the allotted time has passed.
Our days are numbered; this life won't last!

I miss my friend who went away
Yet I never took the time to say
Why I trust in faith and why I pray;
I would share my beliefs another day

Of the open road vs. the narrow gate,
But now yesterday's gone and today's too late.
Every soul confronts its final fate—
So settle it now, there's no time to wait.

I was just like you when I had no clue
Of who and what I belong to.
I lived my life as a game of chance,
A victim to endless circumstance.

Those cunning ways I got ahead
Kept me among the living dead,
Living my life by my own accord.
When a friend shared something
That he'd read . . .
"The beginning of knowledge
Is fear of the Lord."
But I had my own brand of wisdom instead!

He handed me an old torn book
And persuaded me to take a look.
I'd heard of God's great Word before—
Still another thing I would ignore.

Those dark, confusing, ancient pages
Surely weren't written for me!
It has satisfied God's own for ages
(I used to always disagree!).

So I set out to disprove it:
The Word of God is just old rules;
I know all that I need to know,
I've done my time in many schools.

Reading the gospel, it came alive,
Sparking something deep inside,
Shutting out my worldly pride,
Like a living, breathing, road map guide.
If I repent my ways, submit to love,
Grace for me won't be denied!

Many promises by faith I've found;
I didn't know I was so loved.
God has plans, so true and sound—
He broke the chains that kept me bound!
I had to ask, change, and believe,
Reject the powers that deceive!

Now that old Book I know is real—
A double-edged sword to pierce and heal,

Compelling journey through history,
Loaded with truth I was missing.
I dismissed it as a mystery.
But what a gift, and what a blessing!

This new Book now I can't put down,
And so I spread the news around.
The example set, I try to be—
And thanks to Christ, I really am—
Your brand new me!

What We Deserve

That day will surely come
When our judgment will be done.
That time will be here soon,
Though we're not to live in fear.
It will all become so clear,
Sure as morning turns to noon.

It will be too late to change;
The time to wake up is now.
Never has nothing been so real
When no more time is left to steal.
Every tongue will at last confess
And every knee shall bow

To the King of kings,
The living Lord above all things,
Whose tomorrow is today.
By His will alone He does allow—
Just who are we to disobey?

Just look throughout creation and see
How small we really are.
Why do we expect a tomorrow
And don't pay back what we borrow?
(That mind-set won't get us far!)

Another breath isn't guaranteed—
Not reaping a plentiful harvest?
It's time to plant a better seed:

Pray and praise when times are good,
Not just in times of need.

Give to those who ask of you,
Put away your worldly greed;
Life never follows a line that's straight—
Our roads will always bend and curve.

In the end—which never ends—
We'll receive just what we deserve.

Mind Conversion

I really had no idea—
I must have missed every clue.
I thought I knew it all, but
I knew nothing till I met You.

You've been waiting for me, Lord.
Having been here all along.
How is it I denied You?
Now I know that I belong.

The world had been my compass;
In the culture I fit in—
A front-row seat on that long black train,
Companion to every sin.

I was with the "in crowd";
I thought they were my friends.
When You broke me, though, I finally bowed:
Without Your perfect guidance
My dreams were all dead ends.

How did I live just for myself?
How did the things with meaning
Just end up upon the shelf?
I walked alone with my eyes closed,
But through You now I see:
I'll live my life by Your good plan,
The way I was born to be.

Daniel J. Mocadlo 91

For money was my master—
Judged success by all my toys—
(Oh what a fool I was)!
But now I praise God and rejoice!
So open up your needing heart;
Make room for Jesus' loving voice.

Eternity's at stake!
Now I will die awake;
Wisdom's perfect choice
It's the only one to make.

Jump aboard and join the song—
God's dear grace can't be replaced
And life on earth won't last too long.
Join the Spirit, trust in faith,
Believe and know He's in control.
Cooperation brings me joy
For He's the longing within my soul.

I am nothing without You!
My blessings now I see—
Restoration for my family.

I give away so I can keep
And there's no problem that's too deep
That I can't handle without You.
Your essence is forever true.
Sin is always in my sights—
Yet to walk in faith is what I'll do.

God in Control

Like waves move through the ocean
(Who tells them where to go?),
Or like the leaves upon the trees
That dance as the wind does blow . . .
Who directs the clouds to pour out rain
Or sends lightning to its place?
Who measured out the span of land
Or sets the challenges we face?
To those who don't, they should embrace.
Our names in the Book He won't erase;
He plants the dreams that we all chase.

It's all controlled by G.P.S.
Who can match the will of wisdom,
Grant authority to bless?
I can't keep a song in rhythm.
I am vulnerable, I confess,
Submission it provides true rest
In God's Positioning System.

I don't have all the answers;
I live every day on faith.
For I won't take any chances
When everything's at stake.
I rely on my Spirit instincts
And I learn from each mistake.

I pray to follow on the path—
The one to where God needs me,

Not knowing where I'm going
Or how I'm somehow growing.
Please renew my heart and lead me.

Oh Spirit, keep me wide awake,
Remind me how to love;
An example of me, Lord, please make.

Search now and know me, Lord.
I ask Your gift of wisdom
To conquer all my daily fears,
Enduring through these trying years
To finish anywhere within
God's Positioning System!

Love, Significance, and Security

We live here for a reason,
In case you were in doubt.
Many years are like one season,
Recurring needs within, without—
The needs we have in common
That each one of us shares.

We long to be significant,
To be noticed by someone.
We like when people listen to us.
Like our existence makes some sense
Even though our background borders
A completely different fence.

Security is another goal
We hate to live without.
It's the longing of the soul
Beyond a shadow of a doubt.
Security permits us to put worried thoughts aside,
Fearing not what tomorrow will bring.
It can put aside our worldly pride
And grant contentment in anything.

Yet most of all there's love
(Please don't deny you need to feel
This emotion sent down from above,
The only power to truly heal).
For love is patient, love is kind,
It separates our souls from sin—

The missing piece we need to find
For the faithful journey to begin.

Love doesn't sit still;
It's productive in action,
Changing empty to full,
Beacon of satisfaction.

God at Work

When I was leaning on myself
No answer came to empty prayer.
I had my faith upon the shelf
Until God broke me, layer by layer,

To the point of nowhere left to run
Where all my walls came crashing down.
On my knees I was so undone
I gave my heart back to the One
Who set the stars beyond the sun.

My best friend I did finally find—
Though He had been here all along,
The One who gives reason for every love song.
Now by the renewing of my mind
He gives me sight—no longer blind.
Our partnership grows well defined.

God is in no way done
Pruning the weeds from my heart,
No person is so impossibly bad
To be denied a brand new start.

When I feel alone I look ahead;
He walks first in front of me.
To left or right I will not sway,
I won't let fear get in my way;
His promises keep me well fed.

We can commune the whole day long;
No matter how far I'm from home
I've got a trusting friend who's there
Without my picking up the phone.

In the flame I will not burn;
God's purging fire cleanses me.
I'm in His training, challenging and bold;
By the time my refiner is done with me,
I'll reflect His image as purified gold.

For He is there to hold my heart
(The strongest love I've ever felt).
My future's spelled out in His chart.
I know He spoke the world in place
As now He speaks to me,
Not in a worldly manner—
I don't need to wave a banner—
His voice is real as real can be.

Although I'm still a sinner
Through His grace, I am the winner.
He's not just there for the old souls;
Everyone's a new beginner.

To be born again,
To have hope within,
When things go bad, it's not so sad;
I trust then in his faithful plan
For He is God and I just man.

I believe in much I cannot see
(Secure my place in His monarchy).
I'm living in my own right time,
Was put here in this place
To share God's mercy and His grace.
Don't reach out just to touch His hand—
Reach out to touch His face!

All living, let me share: I know
His kingdom's up above—
And never doubt it's here below!
It's best to set an example high
In helping others to reach the sky.

Affliction breeds endurance
(I call it live and learn).
For godly character we must build
And through Christ's wisdom we discern.

Daniel J. Mocadlo   99

God's Word

How fortunate I really am—
It's not to do with luck or fate.
I know that I am truly blessed
Though I'm still faced with many a test,
Secure in my future, no matter the date.

God's promises give supernatural rest.
He delivers within the realm of trust—
A relation with Him is simply a must.

I learn to walk and where to stand;
I welcome challenge and reprimand.
My house on a rock, not built on the sand,
I pray for His grace I cannot demand—
The mercy of God from His outstretched hand.

I'm made aware of right from wrong;
I'm never alone, as to God I belong.
He alone conquered death—sing a victory song!
My yoke is weak, but His love is strong.

There is a place where my spirit gets stirred,
The place to come to be truly cured.
The clearest vision that never gets blurred,
The most powerful message that's ever been heard;
The righteous path will not be disturbed.

Through sixty-six books, over four thousand years,
The message reflects, consistent as mirrors,

The road to redemption, the way to salvation.
Every word is inspired; it's still conquering fears—
The living tissue for drying our tears!

Life's blueprints, schematics, and wiring guide
Revealing all that's kept hidden inside,
Plans, maps, and charts to push pride aside:
This owners' manual won't be deferred,
The one timeless standard—we call it God's Word!

In the beginning was the Word
And the Word was with God
And the Word was God
And the Word became flesh.

Way back in Genesis we see
God, Son, and Spirit: Trinity.
"Let's make man in 'Our image,'
According to 'Our likeness.'"

Our Lord personifies the Word—
The living Word of life,
The message that first must be heard.
The Spirit helps us understand
God's Law and His prophets
And the grace of His hand.

The Scriptures have been written down
So we may believe that Jesus is Christ,
God's Son, with Spirit in woman conceived.
Everlasting life by no other name—
I'm chosen by God: therein lies my fame!

God's Word is His powerful self-expression
Of wisdom, creation, and revelation.
God's Word manifest as a human being,
Restoring the vision of eyes never seeing.

Jesus Christ, the Lamb of salvation,
Fulfilled the Old Testament Law.
His sacrifice that restored our peace
Was full and sufficient despite mankind's fall.

For no true prophecy, we know,
Was ever made by human will.
No, men moved by the Spirit
(Divine duties to fulfill).
Blessed all of us who thirst to hear it,
Who cherish the way of His will.

The truth in Scripture convicts our hearts.
We can never reprove its difficult parts.
It's me, just me who doesn't know
The path of wisdom, the right way to go.
But fear of God helps me understand
What my own wisdom alone can't comprehend;
His word speaks to my heart as a friend.

The source of light for my spiritual walk
Gives me comfort and courage each day.
The power it holds is my delight;
I stand firmly held within His might—
He leads me in the truthful way.

For this, the standard of teaching,
The root of all worthy preaching,
Restores my weary soul
And keeps my fears at bay;
God's quiet voice still leads my way.

Your commandments make me wiser
Than the enemy at my door.
My spiritual shield and advisor,
Your love is forever mine . . . and more.

Than my teachers I have more insight;
Your commands, they are perfectly right
(I meditate on them all day).
Surpassing in knowledge the elderly
With the trust of a child, I walk in Your way.
For Your law is written in my heart,
Your grace to me a brand new start.
So guide me, Lord, in work and in play.

The law of the Lord is perfect,
Restoring any helpless soul.
The testimonies of God are sure;
For He's forever in control,
The simple making wise.
Cleansing the heart, His Word is pure,
A lamp to my feet, a light to my path—
That Word is truth, my only cure.

Scripture more than rebukes wrong behavior;
It points the way back to the Savior.

God's Word makes us wise for salvation—
Through faith in God's Christ we're included
As heirs in His forever nation.

If today you hear His voice,
Please harden not your heart.
Take God at His own Word,
Repent, and start a brand new chart.

Men's words hurt, but God's words heal;
I shall run the way of Your commands.
Your character to me reveal:
That You alone are the Holy One,
That You alone are Lord!
The source of new life is the seed of Your Word,
And faith in the gospel just can't be ignored:

Like water, it cleanses my heart of my sin,
Like a mirror, Your Word examines within,
Like food, it nourishes my soul,
Like clothing, it dresses me in truth,

Like a lamp, a light for direction,
Like a sword, a spiritual weapon,
Like a hammer and a fire,
No judgment as God's can be higher.

Revive me, O Lord, as you say in Your Word!
You've founded Your statutes forever.
The sum of Your Word is truth;
Your ordinances everlasting.

Those who love Your law have firm proof
Of hope and peace passing all understanding.
For the grass it will wither,
The flowers all fade away,
But the Word of our great living God
Stands tested to this day.

I wasted so much of my former life,
Bound up so tightly in selfish strife.
Till the Word of God, a double-edged knife,
Pierced between my soul and spirit
When I took a chance to read and hear it.

Through awe and wonder, rain, and thunder,
History, prophecy, healings, and mystery
Knowledge of God—all one day will fear it.
Their worship response to always revere it—
His own holy Name and His Son, Word, and Spirit.

The one and only Holy, reliable Bible—
I take in a little at least every day.
It's filled to the brim with God's promises plenty.
I trust Him for He cannot lie;
His Word will never return to Him empty!

A Parable

A parable, teaching analogy,
Is cast in the form of a story.
Jesus spoke often in parable form,
Announcing His judgment and glory.

A parable has to be explained;
Its deeper gist can be obscure,
Nonsense to the unbeliever,
But to a child of God it's clear
Through Spirit voice to guide and steer.

Isaiah foretold the coming Messiah
Centuries before He was born.
Blessed are we who believe and trust—
Denial gives birth to blindness and scorn.

They hear and they listen but do not perceive;
They keep right on looking but won't understand.
God renders the hearts of cold people closed,
Because they deny His powerful grace
Offered to all with outstretched hand.

True hearing and vision are spiritual gifts;
So return now to God for your healing.
Without His anchor we sway and drift
And follow whatever whim we find appealing.

The good news, the gospel of Jesus Christ,
Records this revealing parable:

A sower went out to sow some seeds
But some fell along the roadside nearby.
What wasn't trampled the birds ate up
For the pathway was hardened and dry.

Other seed fell on the rocky ground
(The soil didn't go down deep).
It sprang up quick—'til the sun got hot,
But then it began to wither and weep.
A deep, strong root this seed had not—
This batch the sower wouldn't reap!

Other seeds fell among the thorns.
Plants sprang up but were soon choked out.
Still others fell on good, dark soil,
And many the crops they brought about.

The seed represents the Word of God.

The seed beside the road
Right where the Word is sown,
Though written there for hearts remains
Untapped, ignored, unknown.
It's heard, but Satan comes
And takes it far away
So they may not believe—
May go about their way, astray.

The seed sown on the rocky place
Is Word received with joy,
Yet lacking firm root for a base

The hearers believe a little while
Till tempting and trouble annoy.

The seed that fell among the thorns
They hear but on their journey sway.
Life's pleasures in so many forms
Choke out the Word of truth each day.
But passing pleasures bring forth, nay,
No fruit of life, no fruit to weigh.

But seed that's in the good soil, those
Who let the Word root in their heart,
They hold it close and live it out—
They bear good fruit that's off the chart!

The Beatitudes

Life itself is an unexplainable gift;
In fear and wonder we're all made,
Knit, woven inside our mother's womb
(God's invisible hand makes no mistake).

We will suffer trials in this world—
That's how we're shaped and built and grow.
But have no fear, Christ conquered the world.
He selects His own—His voice we know!

The world's system only goes one way;
As God's children follow another.
So know and trust what you believe;
Stand firm and never doubt your Brother.

Favored by God are those who are blessed,
The ones who grasp this fallen world's test.
Happiness reigns in the hearts of the faithful
As misery consumes the wasteful.

Wasted gifts and chances, time,
Selfish pride ("What's mine's *all* mine!")
They're drowning in materialism
While thinking everything is fine.

Blessed are the poor in spirit,
Bereft of hope without God's grace.
Spiritual bankruptcy, all should fear it:
Without Christ we have no purpose or place.
Those who know they're nothing on their own
Won't fall for Satan's comfort zone.

True comfort belongs to those who mourn,
For godly sorrow brings repentance.
Mourning over our own sin and scorn
Will negate sin's eternal sentence.

And blessed are the gentle, the meek and pure-hearted,
Empowered by the Spirit with self-control.
He helps us to finish what Jesus has started:
Reversing the impoverished state of the soul.

We who hunger and thirst for righteousness
Find it in God, not from within.
Satisfaction will be our possession
And the kingdom of heaven we'll win.

It is the gift of mercy
Only the merciful obtain.
Do unto others as you would have done—
A simple, tough rule to maintain!

Happy too the bringers of peace
(The job no one wants to take),
They offer to sinners for life a new lease,
Loving for Jesus' sake.

Unblemished, free of sin Himself,
He loved me enough to take my place.
Christ set His standards higher than high;
We're offered a choice to accept or deny
That name above all, in time or in space—
Join His team and run in His race.

A Need for Faith

From everlasting to everlasting
Never was there nothing!
How can anybody say
We all exist and live today
By a dice roll of chance,
An explosion deep in space?
So many different ways to dance,
So many dreams that we all chase.

I've never met in my years gone by
Any two who are just the same.
Even with twins you can't deny
There cannot be a duplicate.
We can't create on our own but must
Rely on the Master alone for our fate.

So don't let God's beauty pass you by;
We are yet another day closer
To the answer to our questions why.
We're born to the Master's perfect plan,
Created solely by God's own hand;
We're never to argue with His command
But to obey and give Him glory.
A grain of sand—like you or me—
Yet main characters in His story!

So get up and put down your fear:
Life's more than a walk in the park.
Get out of idle, put life into gear;
Seek the light and avoid the dark.

Trust in what you cannot see;
Tune in to the voice, so quiet and near.
Give away in order that you can keep,
Embrace love while you're here,
And take the leap now by yourself
Knowing you are not alone
And really not that far from home!

For we are never in control,
Although we always want to be.
We're equal, but we're not the same;
We share eternal destiny.

Free will has been given to us.
So take off the blindfold and see
Creation revealing majesty.
I put my trust in my awesome God—
By faith my walk shall be!

Bound to Something

I was always asking why
'Cause I really didn't know
The answers to my questions
All around, above, below.

Every day a lesson learned,
Another bridge that has been burned
With hopefully a new one built
In a place that's free of guilt
That wraps us all around.
For here and now and always
To something we're all bound!

Why is it that so many hearts
Rarely ever listen
To that majestic, silent sound
Of the One who walks before us,
The One who spoke the very ground?
When will I stop asking why?

It's hard to trust, hard to deny
That I do not belong to me.
But I could never touch the sky
Nor give sight to a blinded eye.

I'll never prosper on my own;
My strength just doesn't come from me.
I draw it from the love of God
Whose Spirit dwells inside me!

The Case

Things don't always go as we plan:
I accept this fact as a common man.
In truth, though, I'm not common at all—
I'm a child of God and I've answered His call.
I still often stumble; I trip and I fall,
Yet I'm under His grace and I'm led by His law.

I searched my soul and made a big choice:
Do I make and follow my own heart's rules
Or follow my Father's voice?
I looked in my heart and chose a new start—
A partnership forever; we're never apart.

Our decisions have consequences
Like boundaries from fences.
I pray for truth we can recognize
(There's more at stake than we realize—
The end's not the time for a sobering surprise!).

Two kingdoms in conflict each hour and each day—
We draw from the Power we choose to obey!

I praise my God now, Who has opened my eyes.
I've lost my mask and dropped my disguise—
Not given a free pass on difficult things
Yet what a grand gift God's security brings.
My soul, triumphant, joyfully sings!

Yes, Jesus who saved a sinner like me
Is preparing my place for eternity.

How easy it is to wake up these days
No longer in bondage to worry or doubt
With new nature, outlook, and also new heart;
How sad God and I had lived so long apart!

I can't comprehend the mind of God;
'Cause He is He and I am not.
What He allows is all I've got.
From my own answers I will not get my fill;
I must seek the counsel of His own good will.

This is so very hard to understand
From the point of view of the common man,
Like a TV set that won't turn on
Until it has been plugged in first,
How can we know we need a drink
Till we know how it feels to thirst?

My former condition at best was the worst:
Riding on empty I needed God's fill.
He transformed me so I could seek out His will.
I daily need more, my life to restore,
God's Word is the light and the truth and the *more!*

How happy I am to be finally plugged in
To God's positioning system,
Forever thankful He found me
On the road where I'd always dismissed Him.

I've got something to say, as hard as can be,
A glimpse of my reality:

I am who I am, through struggling.
I consider it joy when I'm suffering,
Renewing my mind to understand—
I welcome both challenge and reprimand.

After all . . .
I was born without any wisdom at all,
With sin in my heart, a son of the fall.
Yet I knew how to cry and to lie and to stall;
I had to be taught how to tell the truth.
My Father's chastisement has helped me bear fruit;
His precepts help me to stop getting burned
And I thank him for these lessons learned.

He taught me that my life on earth
Is like a single grain of sand;
Eternity in contrast like
A long white beach's stretching span.

To put all this in perspective
Who can comprehend forever?
Where we end up is reflective
Not of good works we put in
For we're never free from sin—
No, to walk by faith is what I'll do,
Grace provided by Jesus and all He went through.

I imagined an exclusive club
(You were in or you were out).
For many years I thought so
though I always carried doubt—

Always wanting more, always keeping score.
Now I know the Man at the heavenly door!
Thank you, Lord, for my sin You bore!

He forgave my selfish outlook
And everything I took.
Now my name is written in His Book;
Through faith and by grace I've reached this place.
Yes, my name in His Book of life
He never will erase.

Discipline precedes deliverance;
Suffering builds perseverance.
Run your race with His endurance,
Leaning on Him for your assurance:
Not my will, but His be done
Is enough for everyone.

We who fight to change our way
Belong to the Power we choose to obey.
Tomorrow holds the treasure
To the key we've earned today.

I am a father blessed with a son:
What purpose resides in this little one?
Would I put my guidance upon a shelf
To let him shape and mold himself?

Could I let him grow in his own way,
Avoid direction for even one day,
Let someone else teach him to pray,
Or never take time to love, laugh, and play?

Should I leave him alone and not point out sin
Or stand back and watch without discipline?
His upbringing my responsibility,
The virtuous task entrusted to me.
If I don't nurture him but stay silently still
This self-destructive culture will!

Foolishness abounds even in a child's heart,
I must raise him right, right from the start,
Must teach him he has a lasting part:
To be light in this dark and fallen place,
To rise above and to embrace
The God-planted seed that lies within;
To live for the Lord is how to begin.

Thank You Jesus for what You've done for me—
Pierced through for my transgressions
And crushed for my iniquity.
I know being thankful just isn't enough
And surviving this world can still be so tough,

Yet your example you have set
(You've set the bar so high).
I'll humble myself and strive for it;
Through Your strength I can reach Your sky!

The least I can do is carry Your cross,
To give honor and glory to my real boss.
Chastisement for my welfare
Fell solidly on You,
The perfect, all knowing, all seeing,
By whose scourging I gained healing—

Yes me, the sheep who went astray
And followed my own selfish way.
Though I've sinned, falling short of Your glory,
Your amazing grace includes me
In Your never-ending story.

For only God's own grand design
Could save a wretched heart like mine!
Jesus, my own intercessor
Covered me, the great transgressor!

You bore for me my every sin
(I bear Your righteousness within!)—
A partnership You did begin.
Even if I finish last
I'm on your team, and it's a win!

God treated Jesus like sinful old me
And He will reward me just like sinless Him!
To follow Your lead is the least I can do;
Your beautiful gospel is faithfully true!
For love is a product of Your institution:
You loved me enough
To provide substitution.

The Lord who befriends the broken-hearted
Pledges completeness
For all He has started.
He saves those crushed in spirit—
Trustworthy, reliable Friend.
A servant's soul is forever redeemed;

Those in His refuge
Will not be condemned!

I pray, Jesus, grant me your attitude;
Help me live this life in gratitude.
From your highly exalted throne
You sacrificially humbled yourself
To make the Father's purpose known.

You came to earth as God and as man,
Fulfilling Your Father's gracious plan.
Divinity's rights You would not grasp
But emptied yourself, the ultimate task!

You came as a lowly bondservant,
In likeness and fullness of man,
Obedient even to death on a cross.
Through spiritual insight we understand:
You renounced Your godly privileges
And waived Your every right,
Your reputation put aside
Right with Your godly might!

We love because You loved us first;
Conformed to Your image, it quenches my thirst.
Throughout my most difficult trials
Your grace is sufficient enough;
The worst of my sufferings cannot be as tough
As those You so mercifully took on for me.

Born into this world from divinity
Yet author, perfector through eternity,

My eyes in the dark, my director,
My spiritual shield and protector!

I die in Him and live with Him.
If I endure through Him
I will reign with Him.
When I suffer with Him
I'll find glory with Him.
When I persevere with Him,
My tested faith will reveal Him.

By His wounds I am healed;
I trust in His promised glory
That one day will be revealed.

Just what would I do to save one of my own?
Am I willing to offer it all?
As their substitute would I lay down life
In their place to take the great fall?

The actions of love say it all,
Revealing what is hid.
Words can't express my gratitude—
Oh, how can I thank You, Christ, for what you did?

Your promises You haven't hidden,
Your Word is forever true,
Your kingdom is on the horizon—
I praise You not just for what You've done
But for who You are and all You do!

Unable to Redeem Ourselves

I told the nurse, that night she asked—
The night my father finally passed,
The greatest power is found through faith
As you well know, this life won't last.

Dad's pain has now been taken away;
He made the trip home just today,
For God is mindful of His who pray.
Of course I believe; I have no doubt
My Dad had faith within and out.
He left this earth no longer bound,
Already safe on heavenly ground;
What once was lost is ever found.

What once was lost? What do you mean?
I don't know God, but my life is clean.
I'm not a thief (though not a saint).
When faced with anger I show restraint.
Just ask my close friends how I act;
I doubt that you'll find much complaint.

We're lost from birth—the nature of man
Not one is saved by what's within
Until we have been born again,
Not in the flesh; by water and Spirit
To be thoroughly cleansed
And the mind renewed.
If today you hear His voice
Then harden not your heart to hear it.

To sense the still and quiet voice,
Requires of us deliberate choice
To tune in when we need to hear it
And, fearing not, to just revere it!

For no man can redeem himself;
We must acknowledge our offenses,
Leave our sins exposed there on God's shelf
Before Him, turning to repentance.

For those who trust instead in wealth
Find the tomb their home forever.
A faithful choice is a hope-full endeavor.
For who can't see that God is revealed?
His attributes are not concealed,
His power and glory understood.
Look once again at what He's made:
Deny creation all is good?
Ignore the truth—What's the use?
In this we can have no excuse!

We sinners, all bereft of glory,
Are justified freely by the grace,
For on the cross, I tell you now,
Our loving Jesus took our place;
His true redemption completes God's story!

The natural wages of sin is death,
But the gift of God is life, so please
Do not dismiss Him as a myth!
The outcast kingdom thrives on strife,

My God and Jesus I'll always be with
As a bridegroom blessed with a faithful wife.

My dad's real life has just begun:
Called by the Father, saved through His son,
His body will rise that final day
When God's master plan will be on display.
Then every soul will admit and confess
The name of our awesome God alone,
Above and beyond and without the rest!

Like sheep we all have gone astray
But if we know the Shepherd's voice
He'll lead us to our resting place.
Within our hearts he's placed the choice;
Our names from His book He won't erase.

Fearfully, wonderfully we've been made,
Like flowers needing water and sun.
God doesn't wish for any to perish
(He cares for each and every one).

I stood in the pouring rain today
To feel alive and talk to God.
He answered; yes, He caught my prayer
Although the thunder sure was loud!

For a moment or two the sky turned blue
And I saw a rainbow shine like new,
When off in the distance
With an echo of resistance

A 'double-edged' bolt
Came blasting through!

Not just across the sky
(A tear is dripping from my eye)
But piercing straight into my heart.
As I pray again I just ask why
What once was joined is pulled apart:
Why can't we see the end from the start?

Like rain the thunder comes and goes
But in me His heart just grows and grows.
I'll never let those memories fade
For rain will fall on our big parade,
We lose sight, but it is simply true:
For togetherness our hearts are made.

We don't think much about it
Till we're caught up in a storm:
What nature sometimes dishes out
Is hardly safe from harm.

We're just so used to life this way;
We push aside what's close, not far,
Dismissing love, inviting war.
Our promised hearts we have to stay
For you and I are who we are.

For who designs and who defines
How high we set the bar
Or the rules for how we play?
The power in love can't come undone—
Lest Satan victory display.

Darkness Cannot Stand

How do I shuck off arrogance?
Times it's hard for me to do.
I'm blessed in my assurance
That God's will is always true.

I can turn just as a snake bites—
Not on one, but many nights—
Just trying not to wrong my rights,
As angels and the demons fight.

I know who'll be the winner;
For darkness can't stand in the light!
We each were born a sinner,
And daylight's Truth puts out the night.

I know there is a time to speak
But think I should have listened
To subtle signs around me;
God's love that still surrounds me
I kept dismissing . . .
Until, that is, I learned submission.

How could I see me greater than He,
Creator of mountain and desert and sea?
He breathed His very breath into me!
Lord, someday soon I'll bow unto You;
We'll walk throughout my history.
I only hope I'm not too late . . .
God's grace and mercy saved me, and
I know I owe elective faith.

I need to keep my own house clean
For I'm expecting company.
For Your return, I know, is near;
Lord, like a thief there in the night
You'll surely reappear
To take me by the hand . . .
It's only You who knows my heart—
Goliath will not stand!

I'm longing for the sound to come,
Come ringing sure and true.
For now I know the Father
And I met His Son through you!

My friend, I thank you!

Seek, Trust, Pray, Hope

To everyone a different name.
We're called upon but quite the same:
Breathing air as we all do
And needing friendship, this is true.

In each the seed is planted
Yet we take our lives for granted.
So seek the sun, the soil, the water
For many rewards we're called to gather.
Priorities, they surely matter!

A life to feed and grow upon,
Trusting the dusk becomes the dawn,
Each day to God like a thousand years.
I cast on Him my worldly fears
(A thousand years to Him one day)—
One day to give us time to pray
To rise above the ways we sway.
Let down by the world around us
Yet hoping love will abound us,
Though alone our thoughts can drown
Us—Lord, show me my place to stay!

The sheltering rock, it isn't far;
There's firmness there, away from dirt.
God's Word and Son will take us
To our place in love away from hurt,
The hurt that's everywhere around.

All those who wish to keep us down,
Ignoring smiles and wearing frown,
Would drive us to isolation,
To lonely days outside of town,
Pretending that our every mood
Is more of lost and not of found.

Jesus Conquered Death

We're faced with our mortality
Every single day.
I'm glad I am a child of God—
No matter what, or where, or when,
Immortal in His hands I'll stay!

Faith is where we must begin.
We all were filthy, mired in sin.
Our cleansing through the Son of God
Turns every loss into a win!
Forever we're invited in—
Into the throne room of our God.

Repentant heart He'll help restore.
Just know the Spirit's at the door,
The One who guards our lives and more,
The only One we live for.
Dismissing culture here below,
Admission to thrive forevermore
Upon a completed mission—
The final end to every war!

Only through Him is sin taken away
For He alone conquered death—
The ultimate price to pay!

May this be known on our behalf:
He would have died if *just for you!*
We all must follow our Shepherd's staff;

No other name speaks higher truth.
Like sheep we all have gone astray
To live, each one, in our own way.

The end result of wishing
I'll relax and just go fishing!
When life is finished dishing
A number to the score
To when we will be walking
Upon His heavenly shore!

We have not seen Him yet, but still
We're trusting all the more!
Despite life's battle we desire—
As gold that's purified through fire—
Our Savior's true name to admire!
So don't be a denier.

The Spirit transforms old behavior,
Gives our souls a brand new flavor
Then sets our goals so much higher!
We can be a good neighbor
In God's workforce for hire.
Through His strength we'll inspire,
In His promises we labor!

Faith

I trust in what I cannot see
And know His truth is real.
So even when I cannot feel,
When it's so hard to just believe,
By faith alone my walk will be;
Faith is the muscle needed
By every family.

I don't believe that faith is blind
When it's in something we can't see,
For blessed are we who seek to find
The awesome truth in God's mystery!

My faith is based on knowledge sure!
His saving grace enables trust.
The Bible, God's great Word for us,
—Its contents sadly are ignored—
Reveals we're evermore adored.

Faith is assurance of things hoped for,
Conviction of those things not seen,
For by it men approval gain;
It makes our soiled hearts pure and clean.

Ordered by God's Word alone,
The unseen created this visible home.
Through faith alone we understand:
Without belief in God alone
For whom then could we stand?

Noah must have looked a fool
But still did what God asked of him.
And not by precept, law, or rule—
By faith old Abraham set out,
Unsure where he was going.
Throughout an "impossible" journey
This old man kept faithfully growing,
Was promised inheritance and a son;
He'd father a mighty nation
Although his wife had long since passed
The fruitful age of procreation.

Moses by faith left Egypt,
Not worried what Pharaoh might say.
Being fed for years in the desert
Is more proof that faith does pay.
Just who do you know who can part the sea,
Through lamb's blood save a child,
Or tear apart a city's walls
By marching with trumpets—*how wild!*

When David faced Goliath,
Odds were that he would fall,
But nothing is above our God
(Even enemies nine feet tall!).
Or what of Jesus' mother who, by faith
Delivered the savior to die for us all!

These are only a few of the witnesses,
Their stories recorded in God's Word,
Who overcame their fear and doubt
With faith that no one could disturb.

These stories just go on and on:
Few brave people setting armies to flight,
Receiving promises odds would spite.
They shut the mouths of lions
And quenched the power of fire,
Escaping danger, deceit, and sword.
Now walking by faith is *my* highest desire!
The faithful weak became the strong,
Committed to The Lord;
To the ranks of faith they truly belong.

Through faith we gain salvation,
Receive His sanctification,
Encouraged through edification,
Beloved in God's adoption,
Made clean by justification,
Faith brings us God's protection.
So run for His office; receive His election!

Let's run with endurance
The race set before us
With Christ our assurance,
His arms our insurance.

Christ, faith's author and perfector,
Shield for us and our protector,
For the joy He glimpsed before Him
Endured the cross, despising shame,
Secured His place at God's right hand
Beside the throne in majesty,
Tested and tried, and found without blame!

Open your heart to faith (never fear it).
Receive the gifts of the Holy Spirit
Hope, confidence, and joy and peace
Our benefits to own, not lease.
We overcome the world by faith—
This fallen world with all its snares.
Live, love, stand, and walk in faith
'Cause all God has is what God shares!

The righteous ones by faith will live;
Through faith alone we can forgive,
Though faith more precious than any gold,
We're renewed more and more daily
Even as we're growing old.

The Lord's preparing a place for us,
For all who on Him place their trust.
It isn't a matter of maybe someday.
My faith is not an option;
It simply is a must!

Jesus-Centered

I live by my faith—
It carries me around.
Never for me has the lost remained lost;
My found shall stay found,
My future footsteps on heavenly ground.

By grace I've received what I do not deserve
(Christ's mercy holds back what I'm due!).
I'm judged by my God—no, not on a curve;
My soul it rejoices in "all things new"!

Every heart needs to wake up,
To get up and see:
Jesus Christ will come back for you
Though nobody else be true.
Just which of those friends will be around
To answer your crying voice?
Just listen to that gentle sound,
The voice of One within my heart,
For by his majesty I'm bound.

My own existence I can't explain:
It's for one purpose, though, I'm told:
To glorify the God who reigns,
As I grow in righteousness.
As my body grows old
(Despite trials and pain),
My soul will never be lost or sold.

I don't count my time lost when spent in good deeds
Or justify life by my gold.
I search for the seeds aside from the weeds,
For You are concerned, Lord, for all of my needs!

I stopped chasing my chase
When I found You the One
I could never, not ever replace.
You were there all along—
The chorus to every good love song.
My substitutes were always wrong;
God knows I had more than one.

Empowered by His Word, I walk in His ways,
No more do I trust my own strength.
The scales on my eyes in those dark early days
Have fallen, revealing life's length.
With insight I'll follow in God's holy mission;
My eyesight He has turned to vision!

I cannot live my life for me,
Be molded by society,
By many idols, greed, or pride.
Remember, heart, what beats inside!

For Christ takes my anxiety
And every ounce of pride
Beyond what telescope can see.
Oh, who could want a greater guide?
The evil one will be denied!
Though he'll still enter an unlocked door,

The devil knows his destiny.
He may hurt the ones whom I adore,
But I know that evil has an end
And life with Christ is not pretend—
Believer's gift, eternal glory!
Love's happy-ever-after story!

Empty Tombs Available

Wandering past the grave stones
Of so many who have passed,
I wonder, did some really think
Their lives would somehow last?

So many names 'neath unkept grass,
Long dropped from history.
Their stories and glories have all come to pass
But there's no more sand in their hourglass,
The tales of their lives now a mystery.

Time flies and every blossom dies,
Yet every root stays in the ground.
One day they'll all break down, decay,
And never make the slightest sound.

Oh, what a wondrous gift is life;
There's nothing else more tender.
And while we're here our course is clear:
Reflect our God's great splendor.

One life, one road, one run,
One single shot to get it done.
And when again I don't succeed
I'll search for the answers that I need.

I gave my heart to the Holy One
(The author of second chances).
Today isn't too late; we can't simply wait
To learn the steps to all life's dances.

When God called my name I was lost in blame
And quickly running out of flame.
I chose to be on His winning team;
Now He keeps my engine tuned and clean
So I can face my daily tasks,
To take the righteous paths He asks,
To be conformed—this is my goal,
For He set straight my wayward soul.

O death, where is your victory?
For Christ has taken all your sting!
The temporal parting of body from soul
The only consequence death can bring.

My blemishes have all been covered,
And by God's grace I've been recovered,
My former life is past and through;
I'm put together clean and new.
Thanks, Lord, for what You did and do.

This graveyard now seems eerie
As the sun keeps moving west.
These bodies all sleep quietly
(So undisturbed their rest)
Till time appointed on that day
When forever becomes reality,
As judgment pours on humanity,
Our bodies will change instantly
For an eternal home to stay.

The Day of The Lord, "great and terrible day"
(Oh the justice of God that no one can sway)!

Will be great for His own but not so for others.
Did we live our lives for ourselves or for God?
Did we share the burdens of our brothers?

There's just no time to stay derailed,
To live with a negative outlook of failed;
We need to run life's race by faith.
Soon wrath and glory will be unveiled.
Our hearts beat today; it isn't too late
To fill our void and clean our slate,
Gain access through the heavenly gate.

I live to please my Savior
Who soothes my fears of death,
For He alone has conquered it;
My yoke is weak as His is strong.
So sorry, death; please be not proud:
I sing the victory song!

Put to death for my sins, my debt He paid.
But the tomb where Jesus Christ was laid
Wasn't occupied for very long;
In three days' time He rose again
To prove the power of the Father so strong.
He's preparing a special place for me
(Chosen out of this world for eternity);
I believe and in my faith belong!

Time draws ever nearer to my last day
And I trust that He'll take me away
With one grand sweep of His mighty broom

(The same me He knit in my mother's womb).
On that His great appointed day
He'll share with me His glory . . .
And I'll leave behind an empty tomb!

Grace Is Free

It's hard to find guidance in this crazy life
(Everyone has their own answers):
Follow this path, avoid the strife,
And cheat the prevailing cancers.

The question looms: are the paths really many
More than we have solutions?
We tend to follow this one, or any
That promises resolutions.

The truest gift is free for all—
Jew, Muslim, Gentile, Greek—
Our Savior, born and died for us,
Now God *within*, Immanuel,
Still has the answers we all seek.

The one and only path that pleases
The Father's heart, it leads to Jesus.
The Word of God will forever speak
To hearts that confess Him, the humble and meek.

A loving life in tune with Him
Allows His wisdom to set in.
Submit to cleansing from within—
The only way to let Him fill;
Surrendering our stubborn will.

Put God's priorities in view
For He alone makes old things new.

For after all, Lord, who am I
That You should set your sights on me,
That You, Lord, freely chose to die
Providing my security?

I ask, I pray for strength to change
(For with your help I'll rearrange).
I meditate, Lord, on what's right
For nothing's hidden from Your sight.
You separate the dark from light
And I lean upon Your boundless might.

You wait my answer to Your call
(I know that You will break my fall).
I've wasted too much time in grieving
And know You'll knock down any wall
To make sure I, your gift receiving,
Acknowledge You my all in all.
Then may I, by Your grace achieving,
Fulfill Your plan for my new life.

My brand new self no more retrieving
Whatever toys I used to chase—
Those "treasures" that I once embraced
I cannot even remember now;
My priorities have changed somehow.

I can't go back now to that place
Where once I simply took up space,
Drowning in one too many sorrows
Yet banking on endless, better tomorrows
With none to answer to or face.

Knock and the Door Will Open

I see the times are changing;
Nothing much remains the same.
The world revolving around us
Wants to drown us in its pain.

For it denies the answer
To all the questions raised within;
God's seed needs to be nurtured
So our new life can begin.

The One God who forgives our past,
Who welcomes our new future in,
I trust for my redemption lest
I lose my soul to sin.

Because our God is the greatest
Don't ignore Him, play the fool.
His Word the only standard;
Jesus set the standing rule!

I fear history will reveal us
Victims oft and endless prey.
Greed and idols set before us—
Have they made us lose our way?

We believe we're all born equal,
Yet we're hardly all the same.
Free will lets us make good choices;
Still we're fallen, and besides,

Only loneliness and emptiness
This fallen world provides.

God gives gifts to each one freely,
Gifts He touches and fine-tunes;
And our overhanging branches
He alone precisely prunes.

Pray and ask the Lord for wisdom
(You will never be the same).
Seek a heart fit to receive it;
Find your favor in His name.

Knock and God's own door will open.
You will find the "smallest" gifts
Will grow large beyond all measure,
In finding Him, we find ourselves
Simply knowing we're His treasure!

More Security

When have we been so uncertain
That the truth we hold is real?
One man says that "this" is true;
Another's waiting to reveal
A new path to take—the wrong one—
Swearing it's the real deal.

Till we meet the face of facts
Past the shadow of a doubt,
Learn the Word and find a class,
Discover what this life's about.
All are in, or some left out?

Those who never feel the sun,
Those who always turn to run,
Swear our life's the biggest test:
Join the club among the rest.
Our "salvation's" come undone
Missing purpose, goal, or plan,
Missing love, peace, joy, and fun.

Only those who strive to know
Grow to hope and understand:
The purpose-driven life we lead
Comes as true as rock to sand—
We seek God's face and grasp His hand.

The "Way" will never be replaced;
Don't bend or sway to false demand.

Accept His own amazing grace,
For all else, it is just pretend.
So spread the righteous message—
It's the only one to send!

The "flesh" will ever draw us—
Wants to lead within, without,
To bend our searching, stretching hearts
And turn our smile to pout.

Neglecting the seed within us,
Withholding light and rain:
This blinds us to security,
Exposing all impurity.
Denounce the devil's pain!
Just shun it, shield and keep it out
Lest you yourself go down the drain.

For who has ever felt the shame?
Just count the millions like they're one.
To live in fear's the way they know;
To prey on hungry hearts they'll go.
No wisdom means without the Son.
Without an army face the foe?
Consigned to dark and misery:
That's where lost will go.

And who can promise a safe return?
The One who's been here all along.
Why do we sing a lonely song?
Gripping rock we cannot climb,
We put our souls upon the line!

Gain faith to trust and to belong.
The real truth is always fine
Burning as a red-hot ember,
Upholding justice in our mind.

Just is the only way to be—
A constant struggle in democracy.
The law gets twisted as it goes
To highest highs and lowest lows.
What once was the exception
Now we see becomes the rule,
But what about the lessons taught;
And who decides which answers rule;
Who guards curriculum in school?

The faithful bound by real Law
(Nothing directs the mind of a fool),
The greatest folks I've ever met
Are seldom known to be the cool.

God's standard sets the bar so high;
Truth's discipline trumps ignorance.
No more a question what or why,
I live not to stay on the ground
But long to touch the sky!

God Knows Our Needs

I find myself disturbed again;
Sometimes I slip back to this place
Where worry gets the best of me.
I lose sight of my destiny
And need my foot to grip the base.

My base is God, my solid rock.
For in His strength I trust and stand.
Yet I'm tripping on a stumbling block,
Forgetting God's grasp on my hand.

I am His child, I love His law
Though it's a struggle every day.
I still get up each time I fall,
And through His strength I'll be okay.
He's light and truth, my only way;
Encamped within His grace I'll stay!

What else then do I really need?
Why should I fear tomorrow?
God's promises are guaranteed
For us to own, not borrow.

The enemy wants me to worry:
What I'll eat, drink, and wear.
When I'm too slow or hurried
He pulls me back into despair
In that dark, desperate, lonely place
Where worry's much too strong to bear.

I see the birds up in the air
And wonder: do they worry bear?
They neither sow nor store and stow;
God feeds them daily as they go.

Aren't we more valuable than they?
God's glory crowns all humankind,
Yet who of us by worrying
Can add a moment to our lifetime?

Why are we anxious, then, for clothes?
Embrace the care the wild flower knows;
It doesn't labor, toil, or spin,
But Solomon, that splendid king
Was never clothed like one of them!

If God so clothes the lowly field
Whose grasses may not see tomorrow,
Provision for our needs He'll yield
(Thus His protection is revealed).
Without our faith, we'd miss his call:
Our heavenly Father knows our needs,
Not one or some, but each and all.

When I seek first God's kingdom
He never will forsake me.
His strong arm will supply me
Some wants, but first my needs;
His hand of blessing will provide
If I but in his love abide.

So I won't stress tomorrow;
It'll take care of itself.
Each day has its share of trouble,
But I'm never by myself.

Don't Walk Alone

In the beginning, there were no "me's"
Or light or water, ground or trees.
Life sprang up at Your command
Formed and fashioned by Your hand.

I'm the way You want me to be,
So who am I to question,
Complain, or disagree?
I am when and where You placed me!

I thought that I could walk this path,
Could surely face it all alone.
Yet oftentimes I fall apart,
Weighed down by burdens in my heart
That turn my love as cold as stone.

Such a shame they cannot find you—
You are everywhere I look.
I can feel you in the morning sun,
The meadow, rushing brook.
You lead me everywhere I go.

You gave up your own life for me—
The truth the world should surely know.
It's by your grace, yet through my faith
You shape me as I learn and grow.

I grow in love, I walk in line
(I learn new lessons every day).

You ancient of days, You author of time,
The only Truth, sustaining light,
Within Your word I pray to stay;
It guides my feet to walk aright.

The One to Whom I Forever Confide

We are all born within our place
And born to have this very face,
Placed down here for a season.
Who can argue God's purpose and reason?

In this amazing time and age
Who really has a choice?
It's modern times, get used to crimes,
Yet listen to Christ's crying voice.

I know of only One who loves;
I trust in His living Word because
Renewing force it holds within
Revealing to us how we sin.
Without Him we would go astray,
From His own flock we'd stray away.

We're misled when we coolly say
Our private truth we will obey;
In our own strength we'll find our way.
The Lord responds to those who pray
So trust His love; it rules the day.

I've found the news to drown the blues
He's Jesus; follow now His clues.
His gift is grace, not hollow rules.
We're taught to live with falsehoods
Taught us in too many schools.

When I read the gospel it comes alive
(The good news of Jesus Christ),
Igniting something deep inside.
Though oftentimes we still depart
Your grace through faith restores any heart
And primes us for a brand new start.

Denounce for Him all worldly pride;
His grace in us won't be denied.
For by His Spirit's work inside
We're made right and are sanctified.

None is greater than our creator
My personal God, friend and guide,
The One to Whom I forever confide.

The God of Second Chances

He's the One who took my place,
The only One who bore no blame.
It should have been me crucified—
I was the one caught up in shame!

Yet He's the God of second chances—
Not one of us is too hopeless or bad.
He wants repentant, seeking glances.
Its promises like empty romances,
This world will only leave us sad.

I praise Him for His awesome love
That saved a sinner (it was me).
I never dreamed I'd rise above
The angry person I used to be.

Only through the blood of Christ
Can one be cleansed of every sin.
Presented to His Father blameless,
Our sins remembered not again.

I take *His* yoke to get my rest
(My burden as heavy as Jesus' is light)
My sin's removed from east to west,
Forever banished from God's sight.

Not So Demanding

Is now the time to go?
Does this mean I've stayed too long?
When will I ever know?
Is my direction real?
I'm so enmeshed in falsehood, but
To truth I will appeal.

For no one's ever owned my heart,
And no heart will I steal,
Except, perhaps, that special one:
The one I've never met
Or only in a dream—
The one I love and can't forget.

I'm living with the driest feet,
The one's I need to wet.
I'm caring for a wild dog
Who'll never be my pet.

I'm wasting all my precious time—
Or is it really mine?
That time is given to me by grace.
I'm only here for now, I know
(And whom have I replaced?).

Think not of those I follow
But who I'll yet become.
I'm in God's past tomorrow.
I'd survive without the sun
But not without God's Son!

I know that from life's trials
I'll be delivered by His hand.
He's never promised a smooth ride
But only that I'll safely land.

Lord, humble me with gratitude
And share with me Your attitude—
Your peace passes all understanding.
Draw me to Your purposes Lord
So I won't be so demanding!

No Good for Anyone

Why do we carry our anger around
And wear it like a shirt?
Just how can we release it—
All that pain and hurt?

It does no good for anyone—
And good's not who we are?
Frustration seems to follow
Like a stranger in a car.
And when we take it way too far
I know *that* isn't who we are!

Injustice all around us
(I'm not taking all the blame),
But don't we all have needing hearts
For loving just the same?

Our fear will try to rule us
If we allow its presence in,
But don't ever forget forgiveness;
It will let the love back in.

For love is right where we belong
And where we need to land.
Both faith and love, we need them
For they show us where to stand.

To stand against all evil
In its all-consuming forms,
We can't forget the simple truths,
The truths of rights and wrongs.
Each one of us must find our way
To join in the angels' songs.

Fear, Frustration, Pain, Injustice

Anger gets the best of us,
And that applies to all.
I've searched and found the roots of it,
The reasons that we fall.
It comes of our destructive will,
Permitting evil ways their fill.
So guard against it now! Stand tall!

Anger has a purpose;
I face it every day,
Surrounded by injustice
That seems to never go away.

No, I'm not saying anger's wrong,
But still I can't ignore
My need for self-control before
It grows to something more.

For anger would control me
(I become the biggest fool
When I rush to it too quickly
As I know I sometimes do).
I reveal my immaturity
Like I never went to school.

For anger is a friend of fear;
When blind uncertainty draws near
Fear tells us that there's danger here.
Our fear will stop us in our tracks

And whisper untruth in our ear,
Distort God's truth, deny His facts.

I say I can't do what I know I can,
For something just gets in my way.
But still I am an optimist:
I'll push my fear away
Lest I get angry on this day.

Unleashing rage from hurt and pain
Is commonplace in life,
And it can drive us quite insane.
So I'll not focus on my loss—
Then I'll find certain gain.

For I recall the lessons learned
(I missed them at the time).
Too often I'm the one getting burned
For someone else's crime.

Mistakes I've made when I was mad
I normally wouldn't do.
Now looking back, I was so bad—
I jeopardized the ones I love
And everything I had.
A calm restraint and faith-trained eye
Sees wisdom's point of view.

It's clear to me, though, I'll admit:
the tendency I fight
Is rooted not in pain or fright

Or brought about when justice
Is too far out of sight.

It's just my old frustration
When nothing's going right
Morphs easily into anger;
I can turn around and bite.

I know we are too fast to snap;
I see this in my kids
When they don't get what they want
Or they refuse to take a nap.
For fighting nature's call for sleep
Or putting off the time to eat
Can trigger one more anger trap.

So fight the fatigue
And strive to succeed;
Put on your armor for the war.
Enemies arrive in legions
In not one, but many seasons.
So know just who you're fighting for;
Keep anger checked, a daily chore.

The Gift

I Thank God for the gift of forgiveness;
I need it every single day.
Those wayward thoughts within my mind,
The ways in which I act unkind,
Encouragement I fail to say.

I fall short of my goals, it seems,
No matter how hard I try.
I promised I'd control my speech—
Was that another lie?

Intentions: mine are always best;
Reality, now *there's* the test!
It's one way with my thoughts at night
(I promised not to snap or bite),
The truth's revealed, though, in the light.

I know, Lord, that I bend and sway;
My kids watch closely how I act.
They listen to each word I say,
Learn from the ways that I react:
I'll answer, God, I'll know someday.

For there's a righteous way to live;
I get too harsh when I'm dealt wrong.
It takes forgiveness to forgive—
My imperfection list is long.

I'm not a judge, that's not my job,
But that's so easy to forget.

There's many a time I fall out of line,
So many things that I regret.

I'll get up and I'll try again
I cannot count my life as loss.
I am forgiven of my sin
Thanks to the One who took my place,
Who paid my debt upon the cross!

Lived for Riches

I knew a man who got it wrong;
I tried to tell him many times.
So many tried to be his friend.
They lined up hoping he would lend
The fortune gained from all his crimes;
He thought his life would never end.

He left this world alone tonight.
Now where will all his money go?
A champion in the finance fight—
I knew that it just wasn't right
And in the fray he lost his soul.

A classic case of self-made man,
Ignoring pain and human need,
His highest goal, his driving plan:
He couldn't see beyond his greed.

He stayed within the legal bound,
However immoral or unjust;
I wonder what he ever found
His stature became his lust!

He lied to all who'd listen
(Epitomized mistrust).
Entrenched in folly and deceit
Left more than many in disgust;
Tonight's his first and final bust!

It's not about just what he did
But more what he did not.
From countless victims he kept hid
His motives—kindness he had not!
And if he once knew, he forgot!

The cold it really burns in hell,
The segregation—*all alone!*
A story no one wants to tell,
A story with a dismal tone!

Judgment prevails on all that fails;
God limits every comfort zone.
The bricks of gold that this man owned
Was simply Heaven's paving stone!

A Stranger Saved My Life

Just who can I depend on
within my times of need?
Whose shoulder's there to lean on?
(It just isn't guaranteed).

I woke up in a good mood
Like I did the day before.
I just had no idea
What today would have in store.

For everything was going fine,
Not much outside routine:
I had my health, I walked in line.
I followed sight unseen.

The forecast said a sunny day—
It would be so nice and warm—
With nothing standing in my way . . .
I faced a perfect storm!

They say it takes one second
For a life to come undone.
I had no thoughts, I reckon,
Past grace, peace, joy, and fun.

But things don't always go as planned.
I wish today were just pretend.
Today my grave needs did demand
A stranger to become a friend.

Just who can I depend on
When I can't depend on me?
A caring soul to lean on
Was there to rescue me.

Take care of one another—
That lesson I have learned,
Bear the burden of your brother.
We're here to help another;
Don't let a bridge get burned.

You could have kept on going
(You don't know me anyway).
But to me you selflessly turned,
And thanks alone to you
I'm with us still today!

Hardships Encourage Development

If I had never seen war
I wouldn't long for peace,
For silence and tranquility,
For firing guns to cease.

And if I'd never known pain
And what it takes to heal,
How would I have built up character;
How else could I be real?

If I had never been among hate
How could I aspire to love?
There's too much anger in this world
I long to rise above.

Patience is a virtue and
I'm learning how to wait.
Sometimes the things I want
I put off for a later date.

I'm eager for my down time
'Cause I have to work so hard.
Life's keeping me so busy—
Tasks at hand at every curve.
I'm anxious for vacation;
It's just what I deserve!

I've learned courage through endurance,
Pushing on when I could rest.

My faith is my insurance—
My God always gives the best!

If I never had my children
(Little hearts for me to love),
What would I know of innocence
Or of the drive to love?
I've learned to set my needs aside,
To put away my selfish pride.
For they're the ones who need me most;
They feed on who I am inside.

What if I never had been poor?
I used to work for little pay:
It drove me to work harder;
My desire made me smarter.
How else would I appreciate
All that I've earned and have today?

If I had not known loneliness,
Been sad all by myself,
I wouldn't yearn for partnership,
My heart up on the shelf.

I stepped outside and found my love
To build my hope with someone close.
Love, best adventure as it grows:
I thought it was too hard to do
But now I share my every dream
And give my best to you!

A Tribute to Teachers

You're much more than what you see,
You are much stronger than you know.
So please give yourself more credit,
Don't allow your fear to grow.
Do not settle then for less
Than where your spirit needs to go.
Reaching goals requires tests;
I call it reaping what you sow.

Children will look up to you
And they will be a part of you.
They will see inside your heart
And remain a lasting part.
Please be strong, then, just for them
For through your eyes they'll want to see
You're a caring, loving person.
When you don't think so, just ask me!

It's a long, long road ahead of them,
But you can pave the way.
There'll be lots of their tomorrows,
All of which can start today.
For every time I think of you
(It's true I often do),
There's one thing I would say:
I have a lot of faith in you,
And the world will think so too.

She stands as a leader among her peers,
Respected and admired for what she does.

She overcame her doubting fears
And she excels in what she loves.

She's known to put her needs aside—
A bigger task at hand—
There're minds to teach and hearts to love—
Her skills are in demand!

Those little ones she's taught
Every year along the way
Are now because of her love
Better grownups for today.
For they have tried to capture
Every grace that she's instilled,
Through the passion she possesses.
With her knowledge, minds are filled
In every one of her classes.

For she has earned a legacy
And many a loyal friend.
The kind of wisdom she imparts
Will never ever end.

Sharing knowledge, proclamation,
She pursues God-given gifts.
She's a champ in education!
Thank you, teacher.

An Excellent Wife

The glory of her husband,
A wife worth more than jewels,
He trusts her mind and spirit—
Hers a special set of tools!

She rises while the kids still sleep,
Concerned about her household.
She takes all on when the waters get deep;
Her strength doesn't rest or unfold.

She praises and smiles at tomorrow,
Ever ready for what it might bring.
She eats not the bread of the idle
But sings what God gives her to sing.

She considers and purchases a field.
Working with her hands is her delight.
Abundantly sharing her gardening yield
With kindness and dignity so right.

Her husband appreciates, saying,
"Honey, you give it your all!
You love me, my Dear, and I'm praying,
Through our joint faith we never will fall."

Always Going Forward

One thing I can truly say,
My love, is how much I love you.
And another: how easily I forget.
Not so much in big but in small ways
My reactions I sometimes regret.

When I'm strung so high on my string,
Stressed out from each and every thing,
On the run and in dismay,
I fail to realize, Dear,
'Till I see the love in your eyes so clear
That life is too short anyway;
We can't afford to waste this day.

It's hard to believe we do what we do
Day after day, somehow pushing through.
It can feel like it's not worth the doing,
But the moment a dream comes true,
Reigniting the love in our tired hearts,
We step back and review all the doing
Our love has allowed us to do.

I try to do the things I say.
(I guess I'm not quite half the man) . . .
I'd like to be twice who I am today,
So my errors I wouldn't repeat.
My dear, you keep me on my feet.
My darling, I can do better . . .
And I'll do my best to accomplish that feat:

To be the best father (I promise I'll try
To give my best to my babies).
One day when I die—and I know that I will—
I hope I'm allowed to watch over you still.

Another thing that I can say:
I hold my family dear.
This fallen world gets in the way;
It sabotages God's values
I try so hard to display.

Though too much time I've lost
In working far from home,
We always want the ones we miss
Until our travel's done.

But here inside our happy home
We'll never face this world alone.
What's here the world can never break,
For our love always takes the cake.

God Never Gave Up

I am content with who I am
And happy with the things I own.
I call myself a lucky man
With darling wife and kids and home!
I work so hard; my job is good;
I'm blessed to be employed.
Beyond those massive taxes
Nothing much gets me annoyed.

For years I slogged through mud and rain,
Was pushed around, misjudged, caused pain.
Nearly losing all I had
I always knew my heart was good
Though many called me bad.
For I have struggled with myself,
Walked hand and hand with failure,
My hopes and dreams upon the shelf,
My part the drunken sailor.

Through mud and rain, through trials and pain
God never did give up on me.
He pulled me from my sinking hole;
I finally paused to listen to
That quiet voice within my soul.

I put my dreams then to the test,
Striving to become the best
Family man I could become.
At last confronting all my fears,
I turned away from coke and rum.

Focusing to make the grade
I found the sun and left the shade.
I gathered all my lemons then
And now I'm drinking lemonade.

It seems that everyone's a critic,
That everybody wants to judge.
How many miles inside my shoes
Can someone walk to make me budge?

Envy is a dangerous thing;
A burning fire it will bring.
When misery calls company
I'll make sure the phone won't ring!

Wasting all your time on me,
I guess you are the perfect one.
I've got my own eyes; I can see
You're pointing with an empty gun!

Just who's afraid of my success?
Another question: Why?
If they've got something I don't have
It doesn't need to make me cry.
Who hedged their bets on David
That day Goliath did die?
Not many put their green on me
When I told them I could fly,
Yet I'm reaching for the sky.
Sure, they have gifts that I don't have
(Remember no two are the same).

Are we putting those gifts into action
Or drowning ourselves in our shame?
The blame game when we're acting lame
Does nothing good for our good name.

We might be seeing clearer—
Cleaning up that dirty mirror—
The search begins within the heart:
Seek God to find your fame!

We Have a Mission

Everything I love is here with me tonight;
This is the reward I've been working for,
For now is the time when everything's right;
I'm blessed with all I need and so much more.

Our God is so mysterious.
Who can figure out His plans?
But blessed are the curious
Who follow His commands.

Who can't see the beauty of creation
Or note how small we really are?
The author of every nation
Sets all boundaries near and far.

Who am I to live this life?
Please take a number and just wait?
Am I a part of destiny
Or victim of a worldly fate?

I don't take risks with the weather
When survival is at stake,
But nothing beats together
When there's more memory to make.

Even if a poem is hard to follow
Who knows it's meaning anyway?
A point of view can be so hollow
Or maybe just too strong to stay.

Here's what I'll say, though, if I may:
I'll encourage and I'll listen.
Not one of us can take for granted
The purpose behind our mission.

But I am always learning—
And my progress never rests.
Passion in my heart keeps burning,
Refined through all life's trying tests.

Tribute to Mom

I am me, born thanks to you—
A branch upon the family tree.
There's nothing that you wouldn't do
(You've proved your loyalty to me).
I've taken so much of your time;
You never count it as a loss.
I thank you now and once again
For your enduring sacrifice.
You're worth to me the highest cost!
You're still my first and favorite boss—
Without you I'd be lost.

I'm sorry for the things I said
Back when I knew it all.
Yet you were there to pick me up
And teach me how to stand up tall.
Just how, Mom, did you handle me—
My brother and sisters too?
Along with our reality
Did you find time left for you?

Now it's my turn to do the same;
Life's circle now has come around.
We're blessed you're still here in the game—
To you I am forever bound.

You give time-tested answers,
Wisdom that's completely sound.
Trusting you, Mom, as I do,
I know solutions will be found.

Daniel J. Mocadlo   183

I model you when with my kids;
The best that I can do is try,
For raising kids is difficult
(There are a million reasons why).
I guess I took for granted
Those roots for me you planted.

In retrospect now I can see
My vision through maturity
Has changed with all the lessons taught:
The meaning of integrity.
The greatest thing I've ever bought
Is stock in love of family!

He Is Big, and We Are Small

The power of the sun,
Amazing in intensity,
Unappreciated in its magnitude.
Little are we who thrive by its presence,
Unmatched and at its mercy.
Away, too cold; too close, too hot
Yet among its companions
On a galaxy map,
It's just another dot.

I can't imagine how it is—
Just how I'm here now in this place?
I do my best just to survive;
I'm grateful that I am alive.
I'm only carbon in this space;
From dust I came and shall return
With a million lessons yet to learn.
This can only be through God's good grace.

The power of the Son,
Unexplained in majesty,
Creator of our own small sun,
The One Who owns the glory!
I'm but a loyal player
In His never ending story.

He breathed His own life into me!
Did I ever have a choice,
And have I always had a name?

Knowing no one else is the same,
I am because He formed me,
Life, free will are His gifts to me.
I won't ignore his calling voice.
I denounce all evil and rejoice!

It's through His strength that I'll get by.
Though in this world a passerby,
I'm rooted where I need to be,
An eager student patiently,
A sapling here amongst the seeds
Avoiding all the choking weeds.
I am so feeble and so meek.
Yet Christ provides my nourishment,
Though never taking from the weak.

No Connect

The wicked will flee
Where no man pursues.
The doubter will tremble
At the blowing of a leaf.

What is it makes things ordinary—
Common to extraordinary?
Separate, other, different,
Superior, sovereign, and pure?
It's the touch of God upon them!
As they are, will be, and were.

Strangers can provoke our fears
In the midst of paths unknown.
Place and time are unfamiliar,
Others strike us as peculiar—
Make us flee to our comfort zone.

Naturally we keep a safe distance
When we're faced with certain threats;
Subconsciously displaying resistance,
Apologetic with regrets.

Is it a problem, how we're wired?
I don't think so at all;
Aloof from those to be admired—
It's mankind's problem since the fall.

We get so caught up and confused
With all our tasks at hand.

We're insecure within ourselves,
Afraid to take a stand.

It's pride that always keeps us
From shaking the winner's hand.
Resistance is found everywhere,
Ensuring we won't stand!

The sacred touch of holiness
Who can deny they've ever felt?
A moment of mysterious bliss
When bolt of powerful fear is dealt.

This fear comes as awe and wonder;
In the face of a perfect storm,
In the wind and rain and thunder
We're delivered safe from harm.

It's as though we're drawn to someone
Yet scared at the same time.
We want to keep our distance
While we yearn to cross that line.

The first response ambivalence—
Conflicting feelings in suspense.
Attraction so fascinating,
Numbing basic common sense,
And fear so dominating
It repels us to a trance!

Revere, respect the name of God,
Exalted over all,

And pray that He may spare His rod,
Though each of us is guilty;
From His standard we all fall.

Fear of life will never
Keep me on the line.
No, I fear my Creator—
The master, the divine!

I cannot bribe an earthquake
Nor chase heart disease away.
A victim of anxiety,
Misjudged so by society:
I've finally found the place to stay.

God invites me to His throne room,
In His presence without fear.
I'm not righteous on my own
But calling on Him while He's near,
I graduate with honors from my earthly fear.

Free Gift to All

Many call me superstitious
And they say I'm too religious:
Why pursue a God who isn't there,
Allowing evil to run free?
Can *His* hand guide our destiny?
And why is this life so unfair?

Sounds like a God who doesn't care.
But just who knows for certain—
Is there really a heaven somewhere?

It's a matter of perspective
(How we give is so reflective).
We get out what we put in,
Preprogrammed from within.

There's a vacuum in each heart.
Where do you run to get your fill?
We so easily fall apart
But He gives a brand new start!
Just submit to God's own will.

Many people won't let go,
Would rather stifle that still voice,
The gentle voice within the soul.
Focus on their worldly plans
Won't achieve a lasting goal.

With an inbred fear of strangers,
We prefer our comfort zone.

We avoid the search for perfect truth.
What's known to me is to most unknown:
So sow the seed the heart needs sown.

For too few of us are certain
That there's a heaven out there.
Heavy-laden, stressed, and burdened,
It's so easy not to care.

But I read of a man named Jesus.
How much more proof did I need?
He was sent to earth to teach us,
As the Savior to redeem us,
Author of each righteous deed.

Trusting Him and His pure Word
Promises are guaranteed!
The bread of life, the root, the seed:
He'll give us everything we need.

Wisdom never yet disproved
Though it's been tried for many years.
The facts remain, the solid chain
Conquering our fears.

He never lied or sinned,
Abiding by His father's will.
How difficult that must have been—
He alone those shoes could fill!

It's so simple to deny Him
(The easiest thing to do).

Pushing Him off to the side,
Relying on our worldly pride
Is our culture's point of view.

Knowing life is hardly fair,
Wasting so much time complaining,
We've a partner through the storm
No matter how hard that it's raining!

Greatest gift that's free to all:
Invite the Christ into your life!
The phone is ringing; take the call,
Put an end to selfish strife.
For the greatest gift He offers
Is His everlasting life.

Why would anyone refuse Him?
To the Giver, this is cruel.
He gave up all on our behalf,
So let's not play the fool.

There is only One to lean on;
Every answer's in His Word.
I am walking, living proof of
The message I have heard.

Don't ask me to convince you;
Simply try it for yourself:
Admit that you don't have the strength
To thrive in life yourself.

There exists the greatest Shepherd
Calling us, the lonely lambs.
Just pray for Him to carry you
And reach out both your hands.

Because He's always there and He is
The only One who can please us,
I'm riding on His shoulders—
He whose precious name is Jesus!

Sufficient Grace

Trusting in God through a crisis,
That's when I can feel Him so close.
I can sense that He's breathing upon me—
He is here when I need Him most.

The love of God is so true!
I take His wisdom to the bank.
He allows the trials I go through
But fills my empty tank.

His power is perfected through weakness;
Through my own strength I cannot endure.
I will humble myself with meekness
For I've learned that He's my only cure.

I'm being molded into something—
What, I can't explain.
But I'm in good soil with sunshine;
I depend on Him like rain.

Jesus knew the way of suffering
And my crisis can't compare.
He won't force what I can't handle
For His grace is ever near.

I won't fear as He is with me.
I won't doubt He's in control.
All things work out for my good;
To work His purpose is my goal.

God is good, so I won't despair,
Fade or falter, for He's here,
And He knows me more than I do;
He is trustworthy and true.

With a faithful heart I seek Him.
What grows old, He will renew.
That which fades He will restore,
For not a weapon formed against me
Can prosper anymore.

When He knocked, I answered quickly.
I invited, "Come on in!"
Just three years before this writing
I felt new life begin.

Now God's grace is sufficient enough
To see me through tomorrow.
I learn and grow when times are tough:
I focus on faith, dismissing the sorrow.

For God doesn't call the qualified,
Those waiting for His task.
He qualifies us when He calls.
Become His own: just simply ask!

For God is faithful, and He's watching.
Not my will, but His be done.
When I fall, He lifts me up;
His great love overflows my cup.
Our two hearts now forever one!

Not Here Long

God, please bless those little souls
You know won't be here very long.
How could You let this happen
To a spirit much too young?

I'd rather that you took me
Than to see my baby gone.
I trust you have a purpose, though,
Far greater for my son.

The pain I just can't live with:
I recall those deep blue eyes
And the brilliant soul behind them
Always real, without disguise,
More radiant than the bluest skies.

In the brief time he was here
He made a daddy out of me.
He taught me and his mommy
How to be a family.

Time, it seems to have no purpose
As it feeds upon us all.
I'll be with you in a little while;
I hear Christ's beckoning call.

I recall that heavy day
Lord, when You called him home away.

But we need him more than You do:
My heart still hurts me so—
It's still so black and blue.
God grant us both the strength
To keep on pulling through.

You taught me how to lose, God,
But a loser I am not.
And every day along the way
I give thanks for all I've got.

I will grab at all the chances, son,
I know you've never had.
And I will make you proud:
I will control my feeling mad,
Overcome it when I'm sad . . .
I will always be your dad.

So hard to see my son depart.
But, oh, the joy within my heart
(I know that joy is you).
You still live, deep within me,
And you are a part of me.
Because of you I'm better now
For loving is the key!

So many things for me to do;
I can't just stop the living.
So often when I think of you
My heart responds by giving.

God, who will guide the lost ones?
Who will help the needy too?
The silent voice within replies,
"That's just why I created you!"

Pain in Separation

If there is no feeling you
Then what are feelings for?
Why did you have to fly away?
My heart holds dear the truth,
The truth we were denying.
I try and try to reach you but
My phone just keeps redialing.
We took for granted always
You'd have one more day to stay . . .
Funny how it is that laughter
Seems to fade to crying.

If there's no feeling you
I cling to memories (they're not lost).
But time it has a way
Of counting up the cost.
Perhaps each day we'll pay a dime;
Life's both a riddle and a rhyme.

If only we could buy some years
'Cause it takes time to dry the tears,
When I can finally stand alone
I'll pray and beg and borrow.
I don't know how to cook for one.
My hope rests in tomorrow,
When that which once was scattered
Is forever joined again!

If there's no feeling you
Then what are feelings for?

Daniel J. Mocadlo   199

You were my all at once,
The one I always will adore.
Someday we'll clasp our hands again,
Our lost years God restore.

Our everlasting life begin,
Surpassing dreams I hold within:
Your faithful promise evermore
To us who answer gladly
God's knocking at our door.

God's Sovereign Creation

What a brilliant idea
To cover the fields with grass and flowers,
To turn the valleys into rivers
And nourish the dry ground with showers.

What a brilliant plan:
Prep the soil to produce vegetation;
Create trees for their fruit, shade, and wood,
To provide us with food for our tables—
What God makes is always so good.

A fantastic idea:
Fresh oxygen, sustaining life.
Days and nights with cooling breezes,
A beautiful partner for man, his wife.

What an excellent plan:
To give us animals, birds, and fish;
To place copper, iron under the ground
To form into tools as we wish.

A spectacular thought:
Giving songbird so melodic a tune
And placing below those billions of stars,
The atmosphere, sun, and the moon.

A practical plan:
Giving us oil to aid us in industry,
Gold, silver, and precious stones,

Daniel J. Mocadlo   201

Beating hearts, a brain, and healthy bones:
Expressions of God's great mystery.

The macro and the micro world
I can't fully understand.
Neither telescope nor microscope
Reveals more than a fraction
Of the work from God's creative hand.

For in everything the eye can see
Just who are we to cast a doubt?
His institutions (church and family)
Foundations I can't live without.

He's provided everything we need;
His word is planted in our hearts.
It's time to sprout that little seed
What starts out small grows off the charts!

The Spirit Shows

Who can say they love the Lord
When always putting their needs first?
Just who will find that living water
Where never again have need to thirst?

Who can say they love the Lord
When we don't give like we take?
Always running and rarely confronting
The end result of each mistake.

So many powers
Whose source is only One—
Instilling His grace in my trying hours
Until my spiritual victory is won.

Who can say they love the Lord?
We love for He loved us first.
Love Him with heart, mind, and soul;
Trust and know He's in control
And find in Him water to slake every thirst.

We care about the outside
When God wants what is within;
He reveals to us our sicknesses,
Exposes our every sin.

And I've found the place to come
So my new life it can begin.
No matter how bad the current one
A gift of grace to be born again.

My strength flows from the Spirit,
From Father and from Son,
For they are preparing a place for me
Beyond my dreams for eternity.
I draw near in His Word to hear it,
To be shaped and molded like the Son.

We believe in God yet deny His power,
Anxious we are for His coming . . .
While living in fear of the day and the hour.
We trust in God, but not completely,
Ignoring His purpose, we live indiscreetly.

We love all that money (it's really not ours—
Nor do we own home, spouses, kids, or our cars).
God's own possessions entrusted to us;
As stewards of His we live under His trust.

Who can say they love the Lord
While paying homage to some other power?
Our idols the core of our every desire,
Taking for granted each precious hour.

We hold onto sin as long as we can
And follow our selfish master plan.
But God in His mercy has drawn me nearer.
When I could no longer drive forward
(Living life in my rear-view mirror)
My vision He swayed, poor eyesight reversed
(Reverse came in so much clearer).

Repentance, forgiveness
What God is about:
My life is a walk by faith.
Leave selfishness for selflessness—
You won't ever regret it; of that there's no doubt!

Take a leap of faith, get off the fence;
The days will come when times get tense.
Stand tall in the truth of what you believe,
For partnered with Jesus, the best you'll achieve.

Jesus Was Qualified

Those forty days in the desert
Had to feel like forty years.
You mercifully spared us the details
And shielded us from Your tears.
Those forty nights Your living hell
Yet graciously You placed Yourself
Right there in our dying prisoner's cell—
All to save Your children
And all because Adam fell.

Adam fell to the great tempter
(That father of all lies).
He's a wolf in sheep's white clothing,
An angel of light His disguise.

That wily old serpent still plays his same game—
Deception, division, destruction.
The author of greed and seduction
Divides us and "conquers" (at times in the Name),
Prompting desire for pride and for fame.

The devil runs a counterfeit kingdom;
He twists Holy Scripture his way,
More casualties and more victims
With each and every day.
One sobering thought I think of
That keeps me from dismay:
We belong to the Power we choose to obey!

The ruler of this world,
The source of our sin, our lies and our pain,
Claims, "No consequence, no eternity.
We deserve all we want (so grab all we can gain)."
Our culture is caught up in this;
We push our neighbor aside to win;
We glorify sin and in it remain.

Like a roaring lion at any hour
The enemy seeks any whom he may devour.
Sin satisfies our fallen nature;
We've self-promotion on our breath.
(Propaganda the enemy's great feature.)
Remember the wages of sin is death!

Those forty days and forty nights
Must have been like a lifetime within Satan's sights.
My Lord, You were starving, alone, and cold,
Yet You never swayed from Your destiny;
Your temptation beyond mine a millionfold.
No, never counting Your love as a loss
You qualified, Lord, to die on that cross.

To prove to me I am Your own
You sacrificed more than all;
Through faith You're still reminding me
My burdens are so small.

You had to prove in Your time of trial
That You, Lord, were worthy as man and as Son,
For We all fall short of the glory of God
Except for You, Jesus, the sinless One!

Who else could have conquered in sin's trying test?
You suffered, my Jesus, without food or rest,
Defeating the dragon in his despair—
You put in his place this world's evil pest.

Worthy the lamb who took all our sin
As far as the east is from the west.
For Christ, You provided the way to salvation,
Included me graciously, Lord, in Your nation:
Only through You I have spiritual rest.

I put on Your armor, Christ, daily for war,
Expecting the evil one's knock at my door.
Be strong in the Lord, in the strength of His might!
Stand firm in the battle with truth at your side.

Our shield of faith deflects each flaming arrow.
The accuser has us in his sight,
Yet armed as we are with the gospel of peace,
His scope for hope must surely be narrow;
Against helmet of truth who can fight?

The sword of the Spirit our weapon so strong,
Where the Word of God takes its root,
Securing His promises deep in the heart—
His faithful believers, we're known by our fruit.

I'd like to remind that ruler of demons
His future resides in the lake filled with fire.
He may want me to join him in misery,
But thank God, He has lifted me higher!

I trust in my great, living Savior
Who forgave me all my past behavior.
I keep alert with perseverance
Until He grants me heavenly clearance.

Heaven

I know a place with emerald grass and trees
(The weather's always perfect,
A breezy seventy-eight degrees)
Where I never saw a hungry child
Or any soul without a home;
A place where thieves do not run wild,
Where everywhere is safe to roam!

I've never seen so many friends
Spread out so far and wide,
Where hearts are filled with faith and love
And loved ones are all alive!

The place we are now in is so full of sin
But we can't let that keep us down
Or we'll never advance, our victory to win—
Maybe this life is just God's test:
We're to feed our souls, love, help the rest,
To tune our heart and mind
To wisdom, to service and kingdom success,
Determined His will to find.

For money's just an object
But we won't find it there.
Our greed can get the best of us
When we've no cross to bear.

Life-giving, flowing waters
From rivers crystal blue,
Lush meadows, lakes, and mountains,
A new home with a view:
It all seems so unlikely—
Though it's possible through You!

Your glory we're meant to proclaim, Lord,—
For this we all have life—
Each one of us is so special,
Each breath and each smile your good gift.
No problem you can't remedy:
Life is rough, but it's no surprise
That You'll wipe away every tear
That spills from our weeping eyes!

A place where the joyous heart freely sings
(Heard by angels and those without wings)
A place that's not too far away;
Prepared, we'll make the trip one day.

So don't be scared or fall apart;
Prepare for your trip today.
Just open wide your loving heart;
It isn't too late this minute to start—
Take that first step and be on your way.

How far will the rainbow take us
When we dare to pay the fare?
My bet is through eternity;
All God's own we will end up there.

There's no such thing as heartache
And all broken bones will heal!
There's no such thing as fallen dreams
Where faith and love prevail!

The power that surrounds us
Is certain and much too great
For evil to take over
For God's love will dominate!
For love will dominate!

Its essence is so strong
And each of us must play a part—
How else can we belong?

Born Anew

The bridge over troubled waters,
The great seam to every sail—
Through Christ we can be like brothers;
In Him we will prevail!

My former life behind me,
For finding You defined me,
Your Word, O God, my mail;
You love me even when I fail.

Through You I'm born anew.
I pray my heart can grasp Your view
On what it's like to really love,
But I'm not sure what I can do
To step up and to rise above.

I study the rose's immaculate bloom;
I waste no more of life's precious time
Focused on doom and gloom.
For Your insight is my outlook,
My wide angle and my zoom.

The Prayer of a Poet

Ask now, and life will be given you;
Just seek, and you will surely find.
Knock and God's door will open—
For He's loving, gracious and kind.
His Word never fails to convict me,
Its beauty and wisdom I see.
I'm reborn, but before I was so low
I prayed only in times of distress—
To a God I had no wish to know!
What made Him answer an address
From someone chilling an ice cold heart
And nursing a selfish soul?

I'm not sure whether prayer is worship
(Responding to the many ways I'm blessed)
Or if it's more of an asking—petition—
A created, to Creator request.
I believe prayer is keeping communion,
The Power and empowered together.
So yielded I don't think to question
Any trial that He calls me to weather.

We like to keep in touch with our children—
Disappointed they choose not to call.
I wonder if that's just how God feels
When we put up a privacy wall?
For the Lord turns his face from the wicked
But the prayers of His own avail much;
When through faith I pursue His direction
He shares blessings that keep us in touch!
He prevents the ground I stand on
From collapse beneath my feet.

He's a refuge for hurt hearts to land on
Without missing the tiniest beat.
It's His wish that not one soul will perish
(That's ZERO when I do the math),
For God loves you! His soverignty cherish!
Just follow along on Christ's path
For His Word provides proven salvation!

Does prayer turn my will to His will
Or move Him to change His own mind?
No spirit beyond His power to fill.
If your heart's lost He surely will find!
I prayed for my eyes to be opened
(For knowledge sans wisdom is blind).
My Spirit-filled eyes now see clearly
His purposes—now from behind.

O Lord, keep me yielded for any task.
Your Spirit, dear God, I rely on
To accomplish whatever You ask.
I pray for strength to live without the
Desires I used to embrace.
I was drowning in sin, but His love won me in.
Keeping hellfire at bay, Jesus died in my place,
And I pray that today I can stay with His pace.
Before I can ask, He knows all that I need
And all through the day my feet He will lead
In His chosen direction each step of the race.

Please help me reflect Your great glory,
For gracious God, You write my story.
I just can't prosper all alone,
But joined in prayer (our telephone)
You take from me my every worry.

In darkness, Jesus wakened early
And found a quiet place to pray,
Aligning with His Father's will—
A model that still works today!

So pray for self, for child, for brother;
Just intercede for one another.
Lord, stoop down to me from your height
(I'm always focused in your sight)
And keep my loved ones safe tonight.
Please prick me, Lord; when I want to fight—
Resist what I would want to do.
O Lord, help me resolve anew,
Surrendering now my will to You!

About the Author

DANIEL J. MOCADLO is a husband and father residing in the greater Cleveland, Ohio, area. Daniel is a blue collar man who earns his living as a local chemical truck driver, wishing life weren't always so busy. Daniel has a high school education but never did obtain a college degree.

He belongs to a good community and has a supporting church family at Parma Lutheran Church, where he has been an avid student of the adult Bible study class. In addition, he enjoys spending time with his family, golfing, fishing, anything pertaining to the great outdoors, and—last but not least—offering his opinion to anyone seemingly interested in listening.

Daniel views poetry as a challenge some might compare to solving crossword puzzles. Coming to a relationship with God only a few years ago, his writing content and focus have shifted from secular to Christian. He imagines "new-life" as a "well-fed" person leading hungry people to food. This is a message for all to hear.